Collected Poems 1901-1918 in Two Volumes - Volume I.

Walter de la Mare

Contents

COLLECTED POEMS
1901-1918 IN TWO VOLUMES

VOLUME I.

BY

Walter de la Mare

LYRICAL POEMS

*   *   *   *   *

THEY TOLD ME

They told me Pan was dead, but I
  Oft marvelled who it was that sang
Down the green valleys languidly
  Where the grey elder-thickets hang.

Sometimes I thought it was a bird
  My soul had charged with sorcery;
Sometimes it seemed my own heart heard
  Inland the sorrow of the sea.

But even where the primrose sets
  The seal of her pale loveliness,
I found amid the violets
  Tears of an antique bitterness.

SORCERY

"What voice is that I hear
  Crying across the pool?"
"It is the voice of Pan you hear,
Crying his sorceries shrill and clear,
  In the twilight dim and cool."

 "What song is it he sings,
  Echoing from afar;
While the sweet swallow bends her wings,
Filling the air with twitterings,
  Beneath the brightening star?"

The woodman answered me,
  His faggot on his back:--
"Seek not the face of Pan to see;
Flee from his clear note summoning thee
  To darkness deep and black!"

 "He dwells in thickest shade,
  Piping his notes forlorn
Of sorrow never to be allayed;
Turn from his coverts sad
  Of twilight unto morn!"

The woodman passed away

Along the forest path;
His ax shone keen and grey
In the last beams of day:
  And all was still as death:--

Only Pan singing sweet
  Out of Earth's fragrant shade;
I dreamed his eyes to meet,
And found but shadow laid
  Before my tired feet.

Comes no more dawn to me,
  Nor bird of open skies.
Only his woods' deep gloom I see
  Till, at the end of all, shall rise,
Afar and tranquilly,
Death's stretching sea.

THE CHILDREN OF STARE

Winter is fallen early
  On the house of Stare;
Birds in reverberating flocks
  Haunt its ancestral box;
  Bright are the plenteous berries
  In clusters in the air.

Still is the fountain's music,
  The dark pool icy still,
Whereupon a small and sanguine sun
  Floats in a mirror on,
  Into a West of crimson,
  From a South of daffodil.

  'Tis strange to see young children
  In such a wintry house;
Like rabbits' on the frozen snow
  Their tell-tale footprints go;
  Their laughter rings like timbrels
  'Neath evening ominous:

  Their small and heightened faces
  Like wine-red winter buds;
Their frolic bodies gentle as
  Flakes in the air that pass,
  Frail as the twirling petal
  From the briar of the woods.

  Above them silence lours,
  Still as an arctic sea;
Light fails; night falls; the wintry moon
  Glitters; the crocus soon
  Will ope grey and distracted
  On earth's austerity:

  Thick mystery, wild peril,
  Law like an iron rod:--
Yet sport they on in Spring's attire,
  Each with his tiny fire

Blown to a core of ardour
By the awful breath of God.

AGE

This ugly old crone--
Every beauty she had
When a maid, when a maid.
Her beautiful eyes,
Too youthful, too wise,
Seemed ever to come
To so lightless a home,
Cold and dull as a stone.
And her cheeks--who would guess
Cheeks cadaverous as this
Once with colours were gay
As the flower on its spray?
Who would ever believe
Aught could bring one to grieve
So much as to make
Lips bent for love's sake
So thin and so grey?
O Youth, come away!
As she asks in her lone,
This old, desolate crone.
She loves us no more;

She is too old to care
For the charms that of yore
Made her body so fair.
Past repining, past care,
She lives but to bear
One or two fleeting years
Earth's indifference: her tears
Have lost now their heat;
Her hands and her feet
Now shake but to be
Shed as leaves from a tree;
And her poor heart beats on
Like a sea--the storm gone.

THE GLIMPSE

Art thou asleep? or have thy wings
Wearied of my unchanging skies?
Or, haply, is it fading dreams
    Are in my eyes?

Not even an echo in my heart
Tells me the courts thy feet trod last,
Bare as a leafless wood it is,
    The summer past.

My inmost mind is like a book
The reader dulls with lassitude,
Wherein the same old lovely words
   Sound poor and rude.

Yet through this vapid surface, I
Seem to see old-time deeps; I see,
Past the dark painting of the hour,
   Life's ecstasy.

Only a moment; as when day
Is set, and in the shade of night,
Through all the clouds that compassed her,
   Stoops into sight

Pale, changeless, everlasting Dian,
Gleams on the prone Endymion,
Troubles the dulness of his dreams:
   And then is gone.

REMEMBRANCE

The sky was like a waterdrop
  In shadow of a thorn,
Clear, tranquil, beautiful,
  Dark, forlorn.

Lightning along its margin ran;
  A rumour of the sea
Rose in profundity and sank
  Into infinity.

Lofty and few the elms, the stars
  In the vast boughs most bright;
I stood a dreamer in a dream
  In the unstirring night.

Not wonder, worship, not even peace
  Seemed in my heart to be:
Only the memory of one,
  Of all most dead to me.

TREACHERY

She had amid her ringlets bound
Green leaves to rival their dark hue;
How could such locks with beauty bound
   Dry up their dew,
  Wither them through and through?

She had within her dark eyes lit
Sweet fires to burn all doubt away;

Yet did those fires, in darkness lit,
   Burn but a day,
  Not even till twilight stay.

She had within a dusk of words
A vow in simple splendour set;
How, in the memory of such words,
   Could she forget
  That vow--the soul of it?

IN VAIN

I knocked upon thy door ajar,
While yet the woods with buds were grey;
Nought but a little child I heard
  Warbling at break of day.

I knocked when June had lured her rose
To mask the sharpness of its thorn;
Knocked yet again, heard only yet
  Thee singing of the morn.

The frail convolvulus had wreathed
Its cup, but the faint flush of eve
Lingered upon thy Western wall;
  Thou hadst no word to give.

Once yet I came; the winter stars
Above thy house wheeled wildly bright;
Footsore I stood before thy door--
    Wide open into night.

THE MIRACLE

Who beckons the green ivy up
  Its solitary tower of stone?
What spirit lures the bindweed's cup
    Unfaltering on?
Calls even the starry lichen to climb
By agelong inches endless Time?

Who bids the hollyhock uplift
  Her rod of fast-sealed buds on high;
Fling wide her petals--silent, swift,
    Lovely to the sky?
Since as she kindled, so she will fade,
Flower above flower in squalor laid.

Ever the heavy billow rears
  All its sea-length in green, hushed wall;
But totters as the shore it nears,
    Foams to its fall;

Where was its mark? on what vain quest
Rose that great water from its rest?

So creeps ambition on; so climb
  Man's vaunting thoughts. He, set on high,
Forgets his birth, small space, brief time,
    That he shall die;
Dreams blindly in his dark, still air;
Consumes his strength; strips himself bare;

Rejects delight, ease, pleasure, hope,
  Seeking in vain, but seeking yet,
Past earthly promise, earthly scope,
    On one aim set:
As if, like Chaucer's child, he thought
All but "O Alma!" nought.

KEEP INNOCENCY

Like an old battle, youth is wild
With bugle and spear, and counter cry,
Fanfare and drummery, yet a child
Dreaming of that sweet chivalry,
The piercing terror cannot see.

He, with a mild and serious eye

Along the azure of the years,
Sees the sweet pomp sweep hurtling by;
But he sees not death's blood and tears,
Sees not the plunging of the spears.

And all the strident horror of
Horse and rider, in red defeat,
Is only music fine enough
To lull him into slumber sweet
In fields where ewe and lambkin bleat.

O, if with such simplicity
Himself take arms and suffer war;
With beams his targe shall gilded be,
Though in the thickening gloom be far
The steadfast light of any star!

Though hoarse War's eagle on him perch,
Quickened with guilty lightnings--there
It shall in vain for terror search,
Where a child's eyes beneath bloody hair
Gaze purely through the dingy air.

And when the wheeling rout is spent,
Though in the heaps of slain he lie;
Or lonely in his last content;
Quenchless shall burn in secrecy
The flame Death knows his victors by.

THE PHANTOM

Wilt thou never come again,
Beauteous one?
Yet the woods are green and dim,
Yet the birds' deluding cry
Echoes in the hollow sky,
Yet the falling waters brim
The clear pool which thou wast fain
To paint thy lovely cheek upon,
    Beauteous one!

I may see the thorny rose
    Stir and wake
The dark dewdrop on her gold;
But thy secret will she keep
Half-divulged--yet all untold,
Since a child's heart woke from sleep.

The faltering sunbeam fades and goes;
The night-bird whistles in the brake;
    The willows quake;
Utter darkness walls; the wind
    Sighs no more.
Yet it seems the silence yearns
But to catch thy fleeting foot;
Yet the wandering glowworm burns
Lest her lamp should light thee not--

Thee whom I shall never find;
Though thy shadow lean before,
Thou thyself return'st no more--
   Never more.

All the world's woods, tree o'er tree,
   Come to nought.
Birds, flowers, beasts, how transient they,
Angels of a flying day.
Love is quenched; dreams drown in sleep;
Ruin nods along the deep:
Only thou immortally
   Hauntest on
This poor earth in Time's flux caught;
Hauntest on, pursued, unwon,
Phantom child of memory,
   Beauteous one!

VOICES

Who is it calling by the darkened river
   Where the moss lies smooth and deep,
And the dark trees lean unmoving arms,
   Silent and vague in sleep,
And the bright-heeled constellations pass
   In splendour through the gloom;

Who is it calling o'er the darkened river
  In music, "Come!"?

Who is it wandering in the summer meadows
  Where the children stoop and play
In the green faint-scented flowers, spinning
  The guileless hours away?
Who touches their bright hair? who puts
  A wind-shell to each cheek,
Whispering betwixt its breathing silences,
    "Seek! seek!"?

Who is it watching in the gathering twilight
  When the curfew bird hath flown
On eager wings, from song to silence,
  To its darkened nest alone?
Who takes for brightening eyes the stars,
  For locks the still moonbeam,
Sighs through the dews of evening peacefully
    Falling, "Dream!"?

THULE

If thou art sweet as they are sad
  Who on the shores of Time's salt sea
Watch on the dim horizon fade

Ships bearing love to night and thee;

If past all beacons Hope hath lit
  In the dark wanderings of the deep
They who unwilling traverse it
  Dream not till dawn unseal their sleep;

Ah, cease not in thy winds to mock
  Us, who yet wake, but cannot see
Thy distant shores; who at each shock
  Of the waves' onset faint for thee!

THE BIRTHNIGHT: TO F.

Dearest, it was a night
That in its darkness rocked Orion's stars;
A sighing wind ran faintly white
Along the willows, and the cedar boughs
Laid their wide hands in stealthy peace across
The starry silence of their antique moss:
No sound save rushing air
Cold, yet all sweet with Spring,
And in thy mother's arms, couched weeping there,
  Thou, lovely thing.

THE DEATH-DREAM

Who, now, put dreams into thy slumbering mind?
Who, with bright Fear's lean taper, crossed a hand
Athwart its beam, and stooping, truth maligned,
Spake so thy spirit speech should understand,
And with a dread "He's dead!" awaked a peal
Of frenzied bells along the vacant ways
Of thy poor earthly heart; waked thee to steal,
Like dawn distraught upon unhappy days,
To prove nought, nothing? Was it Time's large voice
Out of the inscrutable future whispered so?
Or but the horror of a little noise
Earth wakes at dead of night? Or does Love know
When his sweet wings weary and droop, and even
In sleep cries audibly a shrill remorse?
Or, haply, was it I who out of dream
Stole but a little where shadows course,
Called back to thee across the eternal stream?

"WHERE IS THY VICTORY?"

None, none can tell where I shall be
When the unclean earth covers me;
Only in surety if thou cry
Where my perplexed ashes lie,
Know, 'tis but death's necessity
That keeps my tongue from answering thee.

Even if no more my shadow may
Lean for a moment in thy day;
No more the whole earth lighten, as if,
Thou near, it had nought else to give:
Surely 'tis but Heaven's strategy
To prove death immortality.

Yet should I sleep--and no more dream,
Sad would the last awakening seem,
If my cold heart, with love once hot,
Had thee in sleep remembered not:
How could I wake to find that I
Had slept alone, yet easefully?

Or should in sleep glad visions come:
Sick, in an alien land, for home
Would be my eyes in their bright beam;
Awake, we know 'tis not a dream;
Asleep, some devil in the mind
Might truest thoughts with false enwind.

Life is a mockery if death
Have the least power men say it hath.
As to a hound that mewing waits,
Death opens, and shuts to, his gates;
Else even dry bones might rise and say,--
"'Tis *ye* are dead and laid away."

Innocent children out of nought
Build up a universe of thought,
And out of silence fashion Heaven:
So, dear, is this poor dying even,
Seeing thou shall be touched, heard, seen,
Better than when dust stood between.

FOREBODING

Thou canst not see him standing by--
Time--with a poppied hand
Stealing thy youth's simplicity,
Even as falls unceasingly
　　His waning sand.

He will pluck thy childish roses, as
　　Summer from her bush
Strips all the loveliness that was;

Even to the silence evening has
  Thy laughter hush.

Thy locks too faint for earthly gold,
  The meekness of thine eyes,
He will darken and dim, and to his fold
Drive, 'gainst the night, thy stainless, old
    Innocencies;

Thy simple words confuse and mar,
  Thy tenderest thoughts delude,
Draw a long cloud athwart thy star,
Still with loud timbrels heaven's far
    Faint interlude.

Thou canst not see; I see, dearest;
  O, then, yet patient be,
Though love refuse thy heart all rest,
Though even love wax angry, lest
    Love should lose *thee*?

VAIN FINDING

Ever before my face there went
  Betwixt earth's buds and me
A beauty beyond earth's content,

A hope--half memory:
Till in the woods one evening--
    Ah! eyes as dark as they,
Fastened on mine unwontedly,
    Grey, and dear heart, how grey!

NAPOLEON

"What is the world, O soldiers?
It is I:
I, this incessant snow,
    This northern sky;
Soldiers, this solitude
    Through which we go
        Is I."

ENGLAND

No lovelier hills than thine have laid

My tired thoughts to rest:
No peace of lovelier valleys made
  Like peace within my breast.

Thine are the woods whereto my soul,
  Out of the noontide beam,
Flees for a refuge green and cool
  And tranquil as a dream.

Thy breaking seas like trumpets peal;
  Thy clouds--how oft have I
Watched their bright towers of silence steal
  Into infinity!

My heart within me faults to roam
  In thought even far from thee:
Thine be the grave whereto I come,
  And thine my darkness be.

TRUCE

Far inland here Death's pinions mocked the roar
  Of English seas;
We sleep to wake no more,
  Hushed, and at ease;
Till sound a trump, shore on to echoing shore,

Rouse from a peace, unwonted then to war,
  Us and our enemies.

EVENING

When twilight darkens, and one by one,
The sweet birds to their nests have gone;
When to green banks the glow-worms bring
Pale lamps to brighten evening;
Then stirs in his thick sleep the owl
Through the dewy air to prowl.

Hawking the meadows swiftly he flits,
While the small mouse atrembling sits
With tiny eye of fear upcast
Until his brooding shape be past,
Hiding her where the moonbeams beat,
Casting black shadows in the wheat.

Now all is still: the field-man is
Lapped deep in slumbering silentness.
Not a leaf stirs, but clouds on high
Pass in dim flocks across the sky,
Puffed by a breeze too light to move
Aught but these wakeful sheep above.

O what an arch of light now spans
These fields by night no longer Man's!
Their ancient Master is abroad,
Walking beneath the moonlight cold:
His presence is the stillness, He
Fills earth with wonder and mystery.

NIGHT

All from the light of the sweet moon
  Tired men lie now abed;
Actionless, full of visions, soon
  Vanishing, soon sped.

The starry night aflock with beams
  Of crystal light scarce stirs:
Only its birds--the cocks, the streams,
  Call 'neath heaven's wanderers.

All silent; all hearts still;
  Love, cunning, fire fallen low:
When faint morn straying on the hill
  Sighs, and his soft airs flow.

THE UNIVERSE

I heard a little child beneath the stars
    Talk as he ran along
To some sweet riddle in his mind that seemed
    A-tiptoe into song.

In his dark eyes lay a wild universe,--
    Wild forests, peaks, and crests;
Angels and fairies, giants, wolves and he
    Were that world's only guests.

Elsewhere was home and mother, his warm bed:--
    Now, only God alone
Could, armed with all His power and wisdom, make
    Earths richer than his own.

O Man!--thy dreams, thy passions, hopes, desires!--
    He in his pity keep
A homely bed where love may lull a child's
    Fond Universe asleep!

GLORIA MUNDI

Upon a bank, easeless with knobs of gold,
  Beneath a canopy of noonday smoke,
I saw a measureless Beast, morose and bold,
  With eyes like one from filthy dreams awoke,
Who stares upon the daylight in despair
For very terror of the nothing there.

This beast in one flat hand clutched vulture-wise
  A glittering image of itself in jet,
And with the other groped about its eyes
  To drive away the dreams that pestered it;
And never ceased its coils to toss and beat
The mire encumbering its feeble feet.

Sharp was its hunger, though continually
  It seemed a cud of stones to ruminate,
And often like a dog let glittering lie
  This meatless fare, its foolish gaze to sate;
Once more convulsively to stoop its jaw,
Or seize the morsel with an envious paw.

Indeed, it seemed a hidden enemy
  Must lurk within the clouds above that bank,
It strained so wildly its pale, stubborn eye,
  To pierce its own foul vapours dim and dank;
Till, wearied out, it raved in wrath and foam,
Daring that Nought Invisible to come.

Ay, and it seemed some strange delight to find
  In this unmeaning din, till, suddenly,
As if it heard a rumour on the wind,
  Or far away its freer children cry,
Lifting its face made-quiet, there it stayed,
Till died the echo its own rage had made.

That place alone was barren where it lay;
  Flowers bloomed beyond, utterly sweet and fair;
And even its own dull heart might think to stay
  In livelong thirst of a clear river there,
Flowing from unseen hills to unheard seas,
Through a still vale of yew and almond trees.

And then I spied in the lush green below
  Its tortured belly, One, like silver, pale,
With fingers closed upon a rope of straw,
  That bound the Beast, squat neck to hoary tail;
Lonely in all that verdure faint and deep,
He watched the monster as a shepherd sheep.

I marvelled at the power, strength, and rage
  Of this poor creature in such slavery bound;
Tettered with worms of fear; forlorn with age;
  Its blue wing-stumps stretched helpless on the ground;
While twilight faded into darkness deep,
And he who watched it piped its pangs asleep.

IDLENESS

I saw old Idleness, fat, with great cheeks
Puffed to the huge circumference of a sigh,
But past all tinge of apples long ago.
His boyish fingers twiddled up and down
The filthy remnant of a cup of physic
That thicked in odour all the while he stayed.
His eyes were sad as fishes that swim up
And stare upon an element not theirs
Through a thin skin of shrewish water, then
Turn on a languid fin, and dip down, down,
Into unplumbed, vast, oozy deeps of dream.
His stomach was his master, and proclaimed it;
And never were such meagre puppets made
The slaves of such a tyrant, as his thoughts
Of that obese epitome of ills.
Trussed up he sat, the mockery of himself;
And when upon the wan green of his eye
I marked the gathering lustre of a tear,
Thought I myself must weep, until I caught
A grey, smug smile of satisfaction smirch
His pallid features at his misery.
And laugh did I, to see the little snares
He had set for pests to vex him: his great feet
Prisoned in greater boots; so narrow a stool
To seat such elephantine parts as his;
Ay, and the book he read, a Hebrew Bible;
And, to incite a gross and backward wit,

An old, crabbed, wormed, Greek dictionary; and
A foxy Ovid bound in dappled calf.

GOLIATH

Still as a mountain with dark pines and sun
He stood between the armies, and his shout
Rolled from the empyrean above the host:
"Bid any little flea ye have come forth,
And wince at death upon my finger-nail!"
He turned his large-boned face; and all his steel
Tossed into beams the lustre of the noon;
And all the shaggy horror of his locks
Rustled like locusts in a field of corn.
The meagre pupil of his shameless eye
Moved like a cormorant over a glassy sea.
He stretched his limbs, and laughed into the air,
To feel the groaning sinews of his breast,
And the long gush of his swollen arteries pause:
And, nodding, wheeled, towering in all his height.
Then, like a wind that hushes, gazed and saw
Down, down, far down upon the untroubled green
A shepherd-boy that swung a little sling.
Goliath shut his lids to drive that mote,
Which vexed the eastern azure of his eye,
Out of his vision; and stared down again.

Yet stood the youth there, ruddy in the flare
Of his vast shield, nor spake, nor quailed, gazed up,
As one might scan a mountain to be scaled.
Then, as it were, a voice unearthly still
Cried in the cavern of his bristling ear,
"His name is Death!" ... And, like the flush
That dyes Sahara to its lifeless verge,
His brows' bright brass flamed into sudden crimson;
And his great spear leapt upward, lightning-like,
Shaking a dreadful thunder in the air;
Spun betwixt earth and sky, bright as a berg
That hoards the sunlight in a myriad spires,
Crashed: and struck echo through an army's heart.
Then paused Goliath, and stared down again.
And fleet-foot Fear from rolling orbs perceived
Steadfast, unharmed, a stooping shepherd-boy
Frowning upon the target of his face.
And wrath tossed suddenly up once more his hand;
And a deep groan grieved all his strength in him.
He breathed; and, lost in dazzling darkness, prayed--
Besought his reins, his gloating gods, his youth:
And turned to smite what he no more could see.
Then sped the singing pebble-messenger,
The chosen of the Lord from Israel's brooks,
Fleet to its mark, and hollowed a light path
Down to the appalling Babel of his brain.
And like the smoke of dreaming Souffriere
Dust rose in cloud, spread wide, slow silted down
Softly all softly on his armour's blaze.

     *   *   *   *   *

CHARACTERS FROM SHAKESPEARE

*   *   *   *   *

FALSTAFF

'Twas in a tavern that with old age stooped
And leaned rheumatic rafters o'er his head--
A blowzed, prodigious man, which talked, and stared,
And rolled, as if with purpose, a small eye
Like a sweet Cupid in a cask of wine.
I could not view his fatness for his soul,
Which peeped like harmless lightnings and was gone;
As haps to voyagers of the summer air.
And when he laughed, Time trickled down those beams,
As in a glass; and when in self-defence
He puffed that paunch, and wagged that huge, Greek head,
Nosed like a Punchinello, then it seemed
An hundred widows swept in his small voice,
Now tenor, and now bass of drummy war.
He smiled, compact of loam, this orchard man;
Mused like a midnight, webbed with moonbeam snares
Of flitting Love; woke--and a King he stood,
Whom all the world hath in sheer jest refused
For helpless laughter's sake. And then, forfend!

Bacchus and Jove reared vast Olympus there;
And Pan leaned leering from Promethean eyes.
"Lord!" sighed his aspect, weeping o'er the jest,
"What simple mouse brought such a mountain forth?"

MACBETH

Rose, like dim battlements, the hills and reared
Steep crags into the fading primrose sky;
But in the desolate valleys fell small rain,
Mingled with drifting cloud. I saw one come,
Like the fierce passion of that vacant place,
His face turned glittering to the evening sky;
His eyes, like grey despair, fixed satelessly
On the still, rainy turrets of the storm;
And all his armour in a haze of blue.
He held no sword, bare was his hand and clenched,
As if to hide the inextinguishable blood
Murder had painted there. And his wild mouth
Seemed spouting echoes of deluded thoughts.
Around his head, like vipers all distort,
His locks shook, heavy-laden, at each stride.
If fire may burn invisible to the eye;
O, if despair strive everlastingly;
Then haunted here the creature of despair,
Fanning and fanning flame to lick upon

A soul still childish in a blackened hell.

BANQUO

What dost thou here far from thy native place?
What piercing influences of heaven have stirred
Thy heart's last mansion all-corruptible to wake,
To move, and in the sweets of wine and fire
Sit tempting madness with unholy eyes?
Begone, thou shuddering, pale anomaly!
The dark presses without on yew and thorn;
Stoops now the owl upon her lonely quest;
The pomp runs high here, and our beauteous women
Seek no cold witness--O, let murder cry,
Too shrill for human ear, only to God.
Come not in power to wreak so wild a vengeance!
Thou knowest not now the limit of man's heart;
He is beyond thy knowledge. Gaze not then,
Horror enthroned lit with insanest light!

MERCUTIO

Along an avenue of almond-trees
Came three girls chattering of their sweethearts three.
And lo! Mercutio, with Byronic ease,
Out of his philosophic eye cast all
A mere flowered twig of thought, whereat--
Three hearts fell still as when an air dies out
And Venus falters lonely o'er the sea.
But when within the further mist of bloom
His step and form were hid, the smooth child Ann
Said, "La, and what eyes he had!" and Lucy said,
"How sad a gentleman!" and Katherine,
"I wonder, now, what mischief he was at."
And these three also April hid away,
Leaving the Spring faint with Mercutio.

JULIET'S NURSE

In old-world nursery vacant now of children,
With posied walls, familiar, fair, demure,
And facing southward o'er romantic streets,

Sits yet and gossips winter's dark away
One gloomy, vast, glossy, and wise, and sly:
And at her side a cherried country cousin.
Her tongue claps ever like a ram's sweet bell;
There's not a name but calls a tale to mind--
Some marrowy patty of farce or melodram;
There's not a soldier but hath babes in view;
There's not on earth what minds not of the midwife:
"O, widowhood that left me still espoused!"
Beauty she sighs o'er, and she sighs o'er gold;
Gold will buy all things, even a sweet husband,
Else only Heaven is left and--farewell youth!
Yet, strangely, in that money-haunted head,
The sad, gemmed crucifix and incense blue
Is childhood once again. Her memory
Is like an ant-hill which a twig disturbs,
But twig stilled never. And to see her face,
Broad with sleek homely beams; her babied hands,
Ever like 'lighting doves, and her small eyes--
Blue wells a-twinkle, arch and lewd and pious--
To darken all sudden into Stygian gloom,
And paint disaster with uplifted whites,
Is life's epitome. She prates and prates--
A waterbrook of words o'er twelve small pebbles.
And when she dies--some grey, long, summer evening,
When the bird shouts of childhood through the dusk,
'Neath night's faint tapers--then her body shall
Lie stiff with silks of sixty thrifty years.

IAGO

A dark lean face, a narrow, slanting eye,
Whose deeps of blackness one pale taper's beam
Haunts with a fitting madness of desire;
A heart whose cinder at the breath of passion
Glows to a momentary core of heat
Almost beyond indifference to endure:
So parched Iago frets his life away.
His scorn works ever in a brain whose wit
This world hath fools too many and gross to seek.
Ever to live incredibly alone,
Masked, shivering, deadly, with a simple Moor
Of idiot gravity, and one pale flower
Whose chill would quench in everlasting peace
His soul's unmeasured flame--O paradox!
Might he but learn the trick!--to wear her heart
One fragile hour of heedless innocence,
And then, farewell, and the incessant grave.
"O fool! O villain!"--'tis the shuttlecock
Wit never leaves at rest. It is his fate
To be a needle in a world of hay,
Where honour is the flattery of the fool;
Sin, a tame bauble; lies, a tiresome jest;
Virtue, a silly, whitewashed block of wood
For words to fell. Ah! but the secret lacking,
The secret of the child, the bird, the night,
Faded, flouted, bespattered, in days so far
Hate cannot bitter them, nor wrath deny;

Else were this Desdemona.... Why!
Woman a harlot is, and life a nest
Fouled by long ages of forked fools. And God--
Iago deals not with a tale so dull:
To have made the world! Fie on thee, Artisan!

IMOGEN

Even she too dead! all languor on her brow,
All mute humanity's last simpleness,--
And yet the roses in her cheeks unfallen!
Can death haunt silence with a silver sound?
Can death, that hushes all music to a close,
Pluck one sweet wire scarce-audible that trembles,
As if a little child, called Purity,
Sang heedlessly on of his dear Imogen?
Surely if some young flowers of Spring were put
Into the tender hollow of her heart,
'Twould faintly answer, trembling in their petals.
Poise but a wild bird's feather, it will stir
On lips that even in silence wear the badge
Only of truth. Let but a cricket wake,
And sing of home, and bid her lids unseal
The unspeakable hospitality of her eyes.
O childless soul--call once her husband's name!
And even if indeed from these green hills

Of England, far, her spirit flits forlorn,
Back to its youthful mansion it will turn,
Back to the floods of sorrow these sweet locks
Yet heavy bear in drops; and Night shall see
Unwearying as her stars still Imogen,
Pausing 'twixt death and life on one hushed word.

POLONIUS

There haunts in Time's bare house an active ghost,
Enamoured of his name, Polonius.
He moves small fingers much, and all his speech
Is like a sampler of precisest words,
Set in the pattern of a simpleton.
His mirth floats eerily down chill corridors;
His sigh--it is a sound that loves a keyhole;
His tenderness a faint court-tarnished thing;
His wisdom prates as from a wicker cage;
His very belly is a pompous nought;
His eye a page that hath forgot his errand.
Yet in his brain--his spiritual brain--
Lies hid a child's demure, small, silver whistle
Which, to his horror, God blows, unawares,
And sets men staring. It is sad to think,
Might he but don indeed thin flesh and blood,
And pace important to Law's inmost room,

He would see, much marvelling, one immensely wise,
Named Bacon, who, at sound of his youth's step,
Would turn and call him Cousin--for the likeness.

OPHELIA

There runs a crisscross pattern of small leaves
Espalier, in a fading summer air,
And there Ophelia walks, an azure flower,
Whom wind, and snowflakes, and the sudden rain
Of love's wild skies have purified to heaven.
There is a beauty past all weeping now
In that sweet, crooked mouth, that vacant smile;
Only a lonely grey in those mad eyes,
Which never on earth shall learn their loneliness.
And when amid startled birds she sings lament,
Mocking in hope the long voice of the stream,
It seems her heart's lute hath a broken string.
Ivy she hath, that to old ruin clings;
And rosemary, that sees remembrance fade;
And pansies, deeper than the gloom of dreams;
But ah! if utterable, would this earth
Remain the base, unreal thing it is?
Better be out of sight of peering eyes;
Out--out of hearing of all-useless words,
Spoken of tedious tongues in heedless ears.

And lest, at last, the world should learn heart-secrets;
Lest that sweet wolf from some dim thicket steal;
Better the glassy horror of the stream.

HAMLET

Umbrageous cedars murmuring symphonies
Stooped in late twilight o'er dark Denmark's Prince:
He sat, his eyes companioned with dream--
Lustrous large eyes that held the world in view
As some entranced child's a puppet show.
Darkness gave birth to the all-trembling stars,
And a far roar of long-drawn cataracts,
Flooding immeasurable night with sound.
He sat so still, his very thoughts took wing,
And, lightest Ariels, the stillness haunted
With midge-like measures; but, at last, even they
Sank 'neath the influences of his night.
The sweet dust shed faint perfume in the gloom;
Through all wild space the stars' bright arrows fell
On the lone Prince--the troubled son of man--
On Time's dark waters in unearthly trouble:
Then, as the roar increased, and one fair tower
Of cloud took sky and stars with majesty,
He rose, his face a parchment of old age,
Sorrow hath scribbled o'er, and o'er, and o'er.

SONNETS

*   *   *   *   *

THE HAPPY ENCOUNTER

I saw sweet Poetry turn troubled eyes
  On shaggy Science nosing in the grass,
  For by that way poor Poetry must pass
On her long pilgrimage to Paradise.
He snuffled, grunted, squealed; perplexed by flies,
  Parched, weatherworn, and near of sight, alas,
  From peering close where very little was
In dens secluded from the open skies.

But Poetry in bravery went down,
  And called his name, soft, clear, and fearlessly;
Stooped low, and stroked his muzzle overgrown;
Refreshed his drought with dew; wiped pure and free
  His eyes: and lo! laughed loud for joy to see
In those grey deeps the azure of her own.

APRIL

Come, then, with showers; I love thy cloudy face
  Gilded with splendour of the sunbeam thro'
  The heedless glory of thy locks. I know
The arch, sweet languor of thy fleeting grace,
The windy lovebeams of thy dwelling-place,
  Thy dim dells where in azure bluebells blow,
  The brimming rivers where thy lightnings go
Harmless and full and swift from race to race.

Thou takest all young hearts captive with thine eyes;
  At rumour of thee the tongues of children ring
Louder than bees; the golden poplars rise
  Like trumps of peace; and birds, on homeward wing,
Fly mocking echoes shrill along the skies,
  Above the waves' grave diapasoning.

SEA-MAGIC

TO R.I.

My heart faints in me for the distant sea.
  The roar of London is the roar of ire
  The lion utters in his old desire
For Libya out of dim captivity.
The long bright silver of Cheapside I see,
  Her gilded weathercocks on roof and spire
  Exulting eastward in the western fire;
All things recall one heart-sick memory:--

Ever the rustle of the advancing foam,
  The surges' desolate thunder, and the cry
  As of some lone babe in the whispering sky;
Ever I peer into the restless gloom
  To where a ship clad dim and loftily
Looms steadfast in the wonder of her home.

THE MARKET-PLACE

My mind is like a clamorous market-place.
  All day in wind, rain, sun, its babel wells;
  Voice answering to voice in tumult swells.
Chaffering and laughing, pushing for a place,
My thoughts haste on, gay, strange, poor, simple, base;
  This one buys dust, and that a bauble sells:
  But none to any scrutiny hints or tells
The haunting secrets hidden in each sad face.

Dies down the clamour when the dark draws near;
  Strange looms the earth in twilight of the West,
Lonely with one sweet star serene and clear,
  Dwelling, when all this place is hushed to rest,
  On vacant stall, gold, refuse, worst and best,
Abandoned utterly in haste and fear.

ANATOMY

By chance my fingers, resting on my face,
  Stayed suddenly where in its orbit shone
  The lamp of all things beautiful; then on,
Following more heedfully, did softly trace
Each arch and prominence and hollow place
  That shall revealed be when all else is gone--
  Warmth, colour, roundness--to oblivion,
And nothing left but darkness and disgrace.

Life like a moment passed seemed then to be;
  A transient dream this raiment that it wore;
While spelled my hand out its mortality
  Made certain all that had seemed doubt before:
Proved--O how vaguely, yet how lucidly!--
  How much death does; and yet can do no more.

EVEN IN THE GRAVE

I laid my inventory at the hand
  Of Death, who in his gloomy arbour sate;
  And while he conned it, sweet and desolate
I heard Love singing in that quiet land.
He read the record even to the end--
  The heedless, livelong injuries of Fate,
  The burden of foe, the burden of love and hate;
The wounds of foe, the bitter wounds of friend:

All, all, he read, ay, even the indifference,
  The vain talk, vainer silence, hope and dream.
He questioned me: "What seek'st thou then instead?"
  I bowed my face in the pale evening gleam.
Then gazed he on me with strange innocence:
"Even in the grave thou wilt have thyself," he said.

BRIGHT LIFE

"Come now," I said, "put off these webs of death,
  Distract this leaden yearning of thine eyes
  From lichened banks of peace, sad mysteries
Of dust fallen-in where passed the flitting breath:
Turn thy sick thoughts from him that slumbereth

In mouldered linen to the living skies,
  The sun's bright-clouded principalities,
The salt deliciousness the sea-breeze hath!

"Lay thy warm hand on earth's cold clods and think
  What exquisite greenness sprouts from these to grace
The moving fields of summer; on the brink
  Of arched waves the sea-horizon trace,
Whence wheels night's galaxy; and in silence sink
  The pride in rapture of life's dwelling-place!"

HUMANITY

"Ever exulting in thyself, on fire
  To flaunt the purple of the Universe,
  To strut and strut, and thy great part rehearse;
Ever the slave of every proud desire;
Come now a little down where sports thy sire;
  Choose thy small better from thy abounding worse;
  Prove thou thy lordship who hadst dust for nurse,
And for thy swaddling the primeval mire!"

Then stooped our Manhood nearer, deep and still,
  As from earth's mountains an unvoyaged sea,
Hushed my faint voice in its great peace until
  It seemed but a bird's cry in eternity;

And in its future loomed the undreamable,
And in its past slept simple men like me.

VIRTUE

Her breast is cold; her hands how faint and wan!
  And the deep wonder of her starry eyes
  Seemingly lost in cloudless Paradise,
And all earth's sorrow out of memory gone.
Yet sings her clear voice unrelenting on
  Of loveliest impossibilities;
  Though echo only answer her with sighs
Of effort wasted and delights foregone.

Spent, baffled, 'wildered, hated and despised,
  Her straggling warriors hasten to defeat;
By wounds distracted, and by night surprised,
  Fall where death's darkness and oblivion meet:
Yet, yet: O breast how cold! O hope how far!
Grant my son's ashes lie where these men's are!

*   *   *   *   *

MEMORIES OF CHILDHOOD

*   *   *   *   *

REVERIE

Bring not bright candles, for his eyes
  In twilight have sweet company;
Bring not bright candles, else they fly--
  His phantoms fly--
Gazing aggrieved on thee!

Bring not bright candles, startle not
  The phantoms of a vacant room,
Flocking above a child that dreams--
  Deep, deep in dreams,--
Hid, in the gathering gloom!

Bring not bright candles to those eyes
  That between earth and stars descry,
Lovelier for the shadows there,
  Children of air,
Palaces in the sky!

THE MASSACRE

The shadow of a poplar tree
  Lay in that lake of sun,
As I with my little sword went in--
  Against a thousand, one.

Haughty and infinitely armed,
  Insolent in their wrath,
Plumed high with purple plumes they held
  The narrow meadow path.

The air was sultry; all was still;
  The sun like flashing glass;
And snip-snap my light-whispering steel
  In arcs of light did pass.

Lightly and dull fell each proud head,
  Spiked keen without avail,
Till swam my uncontented blade

With ichor green and pale.

And silence fell: the rushing sun
  Stood still in paths of heat,
Gazing in waves of horror on
  The dead about my feet.

Never a whir of wing, no bee
  Stirred o'er the shameful slain;
Nought but a thirsty wasp crept in,
  Stooped, and came out again.

The very air trembled in fear;
  Eclipsing shadow seemed
Rising in crimson waves of gloom--
  On one who dreamed.

ECHO

"Who called?" I said, and the words
  Through the whispering glades,
Hither, thither, baffled the birds--
  "Who called? Who called?"

The leafy boughs on high
  Hissed in the sun;

The dark air carried my cry
  Faintingly on:

Eyes in the green, in the shade,
  In the motionless brake,
Voices that said what I said,
  For mockery's sake:

"Who cares?" I bawled through my tears;
  The wind fell low:
In the silence, "Who cares? who cares?"
  Wailed to and fro.

FEAR

I know where lurk
The eyes of Fear;
I, I alone,
Where shadowy-clear,
Watching for me,
Lurks Fear.

'Tis ever still
And dark, despite
All singing and
All candlelight,

'Tis ever cold,
And night.

He touches me;
Says quietly,
"Stir not, nor whisper,
I am nigh;
Walk noiseless on,
I am by!"

He drives me
As a dog a sheep;
Like a cold stone
I cannot weep.
He lifts me
Hot from sleep

In marble hands
To where on high
The jewelled horror
Of his eye
Dares me to struggle
Or cry.

No breast wherein
To chase away
That watchful shape!
Vain, vain to say
"Haunt not with night
The Day!"

THE MERMAIDS

Sand, sand; hills of sand;
  And the wind where nothing is
Green and sweet of the land;
  No grass, no trees,
  No bird, no butterfly,
But hills, hills of sand,
  And a burning sky.

Sea, sea, mounds of the sea,
  Hollow, and dark, and blue,
Flashing incessantly
  The whole sea through;
  No flower, no jutting root,
Only the floor of the sea,
  With foam afloat.

Blow, blow, winding shells;
  And the watery fish,
Deaf to the hidden bells,
  In the water splash;
No streaming gold, no eyes,
  Watching along the waves,
But far-blown shells, faint bells,
  From the darkling caves.

MYSELF

There is a garden, grey
  With mists of autumntide;
Under the giant boughs,
  Stretched green on every side,

Along the lonely paths,
  A little child like me,
With face, with hands, like mine,
  Plays ever silently;

On, on, quite silently,
  When I am there alone,
Turns not his head; lifts not his eyes;
  Heeds not as he plays on.

After the birds are flown
  From singing in the trees,
When all is grey, all silent,
  Voices, and winds, and bees;

And I am there alone:
  Forlornly, silently,
Plays in the evening garden
  Myself with me.

AUTUMN

There is a wind where the rose was;
Cold rain where sweet grass was;
  And clouds like sheep
  Stream o'er the steep
Grey skies where the lark was.

Nought gold where your hair was;
Nought warm where your hand was;
  But phantom, forlorn,
  Beneath the thorn,
Your ghost where your face was.

Sad winds where your voice was;
Tears, tears where my heart was;
  And ever with me,
  Child, ever with me,
Silence where hope was.

WINTER

Green Mistletoe!
Oh, I remember now
A dell of snow,
Frost on the bough;
None there but I:
Snow, snow, and a wintry sky.

None there but I,
And footprints one by one,
Zigzaggedly,
Where I had run;
Where shrill and powdery
A robin sat in the tree.

And he whistled sweet;
And I in the crusted snow
With snow-clubbed feet
Jigged to and fro,
Till, from the day,
The rose-light ebbed away.

And the robin flew
Into the air, the air,
The white mist through;
And small and rare
The night-frost fell
In the calm and misty dell.

And the dusk gathered low,
And the silver moon and stars
On the frozen snow
Drew taper bars,
Kindled winking fires
In the hooded briers.

And the sprawling Bear
Growled deep in the sky;
And Orion's hair
Streamed sparkling by:
But the North sighed low,
"Snow, snow, more snow!"

*   *   *   *   *

ENVOI

*   *   *   *   *

TO MY MOTHER

Thine is my all, how little when 'tis told
    Beside thy gold!
Thine the first peace, and mine the livelong strife;
Thine the clear dawn, and mine the night of life;
    Thine the unstained belief,
    Darkened in grief.

Scarce even a flower but thine its beauty and name,
    Dimmed, yet the same;
Never in twilight comes the moon to me,
Stealing thro' those far woods, but tells of thee,
    Falls, dear, on my wild heart,
    And takes thy part.

Thou art the child, and I--how steeped in age!
    A blotted page
From that clear, little book life's taken away:
How could I read it, dear, so dark the day?
    Be it all memory
    'Twixt thee and me!

       *   *   *   *   *

THE LISTENERS: 1914

       *   *   *   *   *

THE THREE CHERRY TREES

There were three cherry trees once,
  Grew in a garden all shady;
And there for delight of so gladsome a sight,
  Walked a most beautiful lady,
  Dreamed a most beautiful lady.

Birds in those branches did sing,
　Blackbird and throstle and linnet,
But she walking there was by far the most fair--
　Lovelier than all else within it,
　Blackbird and throstle and linnet.

But blossoms to berries do come,
　All hanging on stalks light and slender,
And one long summer's day charmed that lady away,
　With vows sweet and merry and tender;
　A lover with voice low and tender.

Moss and lichen the green branches deck;
　Weeds nod in its paths green and shady:
Yet a light footstep seems there to wander in dreams,
　The ghost of that beautiful lady,
　That happy and beautiful lady.

OLD SUSAN

When Susan's work was done, she would sit,
With one fat guttering candle lit,
And window opened wide to win
The sweet night air to enter in.
There, with a thumb to keep her place,

She would read, with stern and wrinkled face,
Her mild eyes gliding very slow
Across the letters to and fro,
While wagged the guttering candle flame
In the wind that through the window came.
And sometimes in the silence she
Would mumble a sentence audibly,
Or shake her head as if to say,
"You silly souls, to act this way!"
And never a sound from night I would hear,
Unless some far-off cock crowed clear;
Or her old shuffling thumb should turn
Another page; and rapt and stern,
Through her great glasses bent on me,
She would glance into reality;
And shake her round old silvery head,
With--"You!--I thought you was in bed!"--
Only to tilt her book again,
And rooted in Romance remain.

OLD BEN

Sad is old Ben Tristlewaite,
  Now his day is done,
And all his children
  Far away are gone.

He sits beneath his jasmined porch,
  His stick between his knees,
His eyes fixed vacant
  On his moss-grown trees.

Grass springs in the green path,
  His flowers are lean and dry,
His thatch hangs in wisps against
  The evening sky.

He has no heart to care now,
  Though the winds will blow
Whistling in his casement,
  And the rain drip through.

He thinks of his old Bettie,
  How she'd shake her head and say,
"You'll live to wish my sharp old tongue
  Could scold--some day."

But as in pale high autumn skies
  The swallows float and play,
His restless thoughts pass to and fro,
  But nowhere stay.

Soft, on the morrow, they are gone;
  His garden then will be
Denser and shadier and greener,
  Greener the moss-grown tree.

MISS LOO

When thin-strewn memory I look through,
I see most clearly poor Miss Loo,
Her tabby cat, her cage of birds,
Her nose, her hair, her muffled words,
And how she would open her green eyes,
As if in some immense surprise,
Whenever as we sat at tea
She made some small remark to me.

'Tis always drowsy summer when
From out the past she comes again;
The westering sunshine in a pool
Floats in her parlour still and cool;
While the slim bird its lean wires shakes,
As into piercing song it breaks;
Till Peter's pale-green eyes ajar
Dream, wake; wake, dream, in one brief bar.
And I am sitting, dull and shy,
And she with gaze of vacancy,

And large hands folded on the tray,
Musing the afternoon away;
Her satin bosom heaving slow
With sighs that softly ebb and flow.
And her plain face in such dismay,
It seems unkind to look her way:

Until all cheerful back will come
Her gentle gleaming spirit home:
And one would think that poor Miss Loo
Asked nothing else, if she had you.

THE TAILOR

Few footsteps stray when dusk droops o'er
The tailor's old stone-lintelled door.
There sits he stitching half asleep,
Beside his smoky tallow dip.
"Click, click," his needle hastes, and shrill
Cries back the cricket beneath the sill.
Sometimes he stays, and over his thread
Leans sidelong his old tousled head;
Or stoops to peer with half-shut eye
When some strange footfall echoes by;
Till clearer gleams his candle's spark
Into the dusty summer dark.
Then from his crosslegs he gets down,
To find how dark the evening is grown;
And hunched-up in his door he will hear
The cricket whistling crisp and clear;
And so beneath the starry grey
Will mutter half a seam away.

MARTHA

"Once ... once upon a time ..."
  Over and over again,
Martha would tell us her stories,
  In the hazel glen.

Hers were those clear grey eyes
  You watch, and the story seems
Told by their beautifulness
  Tranquil as dreams.

She would sit with her two slim hands
  Clasped round her bended knees;
While we on our elbows lolled,
  And stared at ease.

Her voice and her narrow chin,
  Her grave small lovely head,
Seemed half the meaning
  Of the words she said.

"Once ... once upon a time ..."
  Like a dream you dream in the night,
Fairies and gnomes stole out
  In the leaf-green light.

And her beauty far away
  Would fade, as her voice ran on,
Till hazel and summer sun
  And all were gone:

All fordone and forgot;
  And like clouds in the height of the sky,
Our hearts stood still in the hush
  Of an age gone by.

THE SLEEPER

As Ann came in one summer's day,
  She felt that she must creep,
So silent was the clear cool house,
  It seemed a house of sleep.
And sure, when she pushed open the door,
  Rapt in the stillness there,
Her mother sat, with stooping head,
  Asleep upon a chair;
Fast--fast asleep; her two hands laid
  Loose-folded on her knee,
So that her small unconscious face
  Looked half unreal to be:
So calmly lit with sleep's pale light

Each feature was; so fair
Her forehead--every trouble was
  Smoothed out beneath her hair.
But though her mind in dream now moved,
  Still seemed her gaze to rest--
From out beneath her fast-sealed lids,
  Above her moving breast--
On Ann; as quite, quite still she stood;
  Yet slumber lay so deep
Even her hands upon her lap
  Seemed saturate with sleep.
And as Ann peeped, a cloudlike dread
  Stole over her, and then,
On stealthy, mouselike feet she trod,
  And tiptoed out again.

THE KEYS OF MORNING

While at her bedroom window once,
  Learning her task for school,
Little Louisa lonely sat
  In the morning clear and cool,
She slanted her small bead-brown eyes
  Across the empty street,
And saw Death softly watching her
  In the sunshine pale and sweet.

His was a long lean sallow face;
  He sat with half-shut eyes,
Like an old sailor in a ship
  Becalmed 'neath tropic skies.
Beside him in the dust he had set
  His staff and shady hat;
These, peeping small, Louisa saw
  Quite clearly where she sat--

The thinness of his coal-black locks,
  His hands so long and lean
They scarcely seemed to grasp at all
  The keys that hung between:
Both were of gold, but one was small,
  And with this last did he
Wag in the air, as if to say,
  "Come hither, child, to me!"

Louisa laid her lesson book
  On the cold window-sill;
And in the sleepy sunshine house
  Went softly down, until
She stood in the half-opened door,
  And peeped. But strange to say,
Where Death just now had sunning sat
  Only a shadow lay:
Just the tall chimney's round-topped cowl,
  And the small sun behind,
Had with its shadow in the dust
  Called sleepy Death to mind.
But most she thought how strange it was
  Two keys that he should bear,

And that, when beckoning, he should wag
  The littlest in the air.

RACHEL

Rachel sings sweet--
  Oh yes, at night,
Her pale face bent
  In the candle-light,
Her slim hands touch
  The answering keys,
And she sings of hope
  And of memories:
Sings to the little
  Boy that stands
Watching those slim,
  Light, heedful hands.
He looks in her face;
  Her dark eyes seem
Dark with a beautiful
  Distant dream;
And still she plays,
  Sings tenderly
To him of hope,
  And of memory.

ALONE

A very old woman
Lives in yon house.
The squeak of the cricket,
The stir of the mouse,
Are all she knows
Of the earth and us.

Once she was young,
Would dance and play,
Like many another
Young popinjay;
And run to her mother
At dusk of day.

And colours bright
She delighted in;
The fiddle to hear,
And to lift her chin,
And sing as small
As a twittering wren.

But age apace
Comes at last to all;
And a lone house filled

With the cricket's call;
And the scampering mouse
In the hollow wall.

THE BELLS

Shadow and light both strove to be
The eight bell-ringers' company,
As with his gliding rope in hand,
Counting his changes, each did stand;
While rang and trembled every stone,
To music by the bell-mouths blown:
Till the bright clouds that towered on high
Seemed to re-echo cry with cry.
Still swang the clappers to and fro,
When, in the far-spread fields below,
I saw a ploughman with his team
Lift to the bells and fix on them
His distant eyes, as if he would
Drink in the utmost sound he could;
While near him sat his children three,
And in the green grass placidly
Played undistracted on, as if
What music earthly bells might give
Could only faintly stir their dream,
And stillness make more lovely seem.

Soon night hid horses, children, all
In sleep deep and ambrosial.
Yet, yet, it seemed, from star to star,
Welling now near, now faint and far,
Those echoing bells rang on in dream,
And stillness made even lovelier seem.

THE SCARECROW

All winter through I bow my head
  Beneath the driving rain;
The North Wind powders me with snow
  And blows me back again;
At midnight 'neath a maze of stars
  I flame with glittering rime,
And stand, above the stubble, stiff
  As mail at morning-prime.
But when that child, called Spring, and all
  His host of children, come,
Scattering their buds and dew upon
  These acres of my home,
Some rapture in my rags awakes;
  I lift void eyes and scan
The skies for crows, those ravening foes,
  Of my strange master, Man.
I watch him striding lank behind

His clashing team, and know
Soon will the wheat swish body high
  Where once lay sterile snow;
Soon shall I gaze across a sea
  Of sun-begotten grain,
Which my unflinching watch hath sealed
  For harvest once again.

NOD

Softly along the road of evening,
  In a twilight dim with rose,
Wrinkled with age, and drenched with dew,
  Old Nod, the shepherd, goes.

His drowsy flock streams on before him,
  Their fleeces charged with gold,
To where the sun's last beam leans low
  On Nod the shepherd's fold.

The hedge is quick and green with brier,
  From their sand the conies creep;
And all the birds that fly in heaven
  Flock singing home to sleep.

His lambs outnumber a noon's roses,

Yet, when night's shadows fall,
His blind old sheep-dog, Slumber-soon,
  Misses not one of all.

His are the quiet steeps of dreamland,
  The waters of no-more-pain,
His ram's bell rings 'neath an arch of stars,
  "Rest, rest, and rest again."

THE BINDWEED

The bindweed roots pierce down
  Deeper than men do lie,
Laid in their dark-shut graves
  Their slumbering kinsmen by.

Yet what frail thin-spun flowers
  She casts into the air,
To breathe the sunshine, and
  To leave her fragrance there.

But when the sweet moon comes,
  Showering her silver down,
Half-wreathed in faint sleep,
  They droop where they have blown.

So all the grass is set,
  Beneath her trembling ray,
With buds that have been flowers,
  Brimmed with reflected day.

WINTER

Clouded with snow
  The cold winds blow,
And shrill on leafless bough
The robin with its burning breast
  Alone sings now.

  The rayless sun,
  Day's journey done,
Sheds its last ebbing light
On fields in leagues of beauty spread
  Unearthly white.

  Thick draws the dark,
  And spark by spark,
The frost-fires kindle, and soon
Over that sea of frozen foam
  Floats the white moon.

THERE BLOOMS NO BUD IN MAY

There blooms no bud in May
  Can for its white compare
With snow at break of day,
  On fields forlorn and bare.

For shadow it hath rose,
  Azure, and amethyst;
And every air that blows
  Dies out in beauteous mist.

It hangs the frozen bough
  With flowers on which the night
Wheeling her darkness through
  Scatters a starry light.

Fearful of its pale glare
  In flocks the starlings rise;
Slide through the frosty air,
  And perch with plaintive cries.

Only the inky rook,
  Hunched cold in ruffled wings,
Its snowy nest forsook,
  Caws of unnumbered Springs.

NOON AND NIGHT FLOWER

Not any flower that blows
  But shining watch doth keep;
Every swift changing chequered hour it knows
Now to break forth in beauty; now to sleep.

This for the roving bee
  Keeps open house, and this
Stainless and clear is, that in darkness she
May lure the moth to where her nectar is.

Lovely beyond the rest
  Are these of all delight:--
The tiny pimpernel that noon loves best,
The primrose palely burning through the night.

One 'neath day's burning sky
  With ruby decks her place,
The other when Eve's chariot glideth by
Lifts her dim torch to light that dreaming face.

ESTRANGED

No one was with me there--
Happy I was--alone;
Yet from the sunshine suddenly
   A joy was gone.

A bird in an empty house
Sad echoes makes to ring,
Flitting from room to room
   On restless wing:

Till from its shades he flies,
And leaves forlorn and dim
The narrow solitudes
   So strange to him.

So, when with fickle heart
I joyed in the passing day,
A presence my mood estranged
   Went grieved away.

THE TIRED CUPID

The thin moonlight with trickling ray,
Thridding the boughs of silver may,
Trembles in beauty, pale and cool,
On folded flower, and mantled pool.
All in a haze the rushes lean--
And he--he sits, with chin between
His two cold hands; his bare feet set
Deep in the grasses, green and wet.
About his head a hundred rings
Of gold loop down to meet his wings,
Whose feathers, arched their stillness through,
Gleam with slow-gathering drops of dew.
The mouse-bat peers; the stealthy vole
Creeps from the covert of its hole;
A shimmering moth its pinions furls,
Grey in the moonshine of his curls;
'Neath the faint stars the night-airs stray,
Scattering the fragrance of the may;
And with each stirring of the bough
Shadow beclouds his childlike brow.

DREAMS

Be gentle, O hands of a child;
Be true: like a shadowy sea
In the starry darkness of night
   Are your eyes to me.

But words are shallow, and soon
Dreams fade that the heart once knew;
And youth fades out in the mind,
   In the dark eyes too.

What can a tired heart say,
Which the wise of the world have made dumb?
Save to the lonely dreams of a child,
   "Return again, come!"

FAITHLESS

The words you said grow faint;
  The lamps you lit burn dim;
Yet, still be near your faithless friend

To urge and counsel him.

Still with returning feet
  To where life's shadows brood,
With steadfast eyes made clear in death
  Haunt his vague solitude.

So he, beguiled with earth,
  Yet with its vain things vexed,
Keep even to his own heart unknown
  Your memory unperplexed.

THE SHADE

Darker than night; and oh, much darker she,
Whose eyes in deep night darkness gaze on me.
No stars surround her; yet the moon seems hid
Afar somewhere, beneath that narrow lid.
She darkens against the darkness; and her face
Only by adding thought to thought I trace,
Limned shadowily: O dream, return once more
To gloomy Hades and the whispering shore!

BE ANGRY NOW NO MORE

Be angry now no more!
  If I have grieved thee--if
Thy kindness, mine before,
No hope may now restore:
  Only forgive, forgive!

If still resentment burns
  In thy cold breast, oh if
No more to pity turns,
No more, once tender, yearns
  Thy love; oh yet forgive!...

Ask of the winter rain
June's withered rose again:
Ask grace of the salt sea:
She will not answer thee.
God would ten times have shriven
A heart so riven;
In her cold care thou would'st be
Still unforgiven.

EXILE

Had the gods loved me I had lain
  Where darnel is, and thorn,
And the wild night-bird's nightlong strain
  Trembles in boughs forlorn.

Nay, but they loved me not; and I
  Must needs a stranger be,
Whose every exiled day gone by
  Aches with their memory.

WHERE?

Where is my love--
  In silence and shadow she lies,
Under the April-grey, calm waste of the skies;
  And a bird above,
  In the darkness tender and clear,
Keeps saying over and over, Love lies here!

  Not that she's dead;

Only her soul is flown
Out of its last pure earthly mansion;
   And cries instead
 In the darkness, tender and clear,
Like the voice of a bird in the leaves, Love--
   Love lies here.

MUSIC UNHEARD

Sweet sounds, begone--
  Whose music on my ear
Stirs foolish discontent
  Or lingering here;
When, if I crossed
  The crystal verge of death,
Him I should see.
  Who these sounds murmureth.

Sweet sounds, begone--
  Ask not my heart to break
Its bond of bravery for
  Sweet quiet's sake;
Lure not my feet
  To leave the path they must
Tread on, unfaltering,
  Till I sleep in dust.

Sweet sounds, begone!
  Though silence brings apace
Deadly disquiet
  Of this homeless place;
And all I love
  In beauty cries to me,
"We but vain shadows
  And reflections be."

ALL THAT'S PAST

Very old are the woods;
  And the buds that break
Out of the brier's boughs,
  When March winds wake,
So old with their beauty are--
  Oh, no man knows
Through what wild centuries
  Roves back the rose.

Very old are the brooks;
  And the rills that rise
Where snow sleeps cold beneath
  The azure skies
Sing such a history

Of come and gone,
Their every drop is as wise
   As Solomon.

Very old are we men;
   Our dreams are tales
Told in dim Eden
   By Eve's nightingales;
We wake and whisper awhile,
   But, the day gone by,
Silence and sleep like fields
   Of amaranth lie.

WHEN THE ROSE IS FADED

When the rose is faded,
   Memory may still dwell on
Her beauty shadowed,
   And the sweet smell gone.

That vanishing loveliness,
   That burdening breath
No bond of life hath then
   Nor grief of death.

'Tis the immortal thought

Whose passion still
Makes of the changing
The unchangeable.

Oh, thus thy beauty,
Loveliest on earth to me,
Dark with no sorrow, shines
And burns, with Thee.

SLEEP

Men all, and birds, and creeping beasts,
When the dark of night is deep,
From the moving wonder of their lives
Commit themselves to sleep.

Without a thought, or fear, they shut
The narrow gates of sense;
Heedless and quiet, in slumber turn
Their strength to impotence.

The transient strangeness of the earth
Their spirits no more see:
Within a silent gloom withdrawn,
They slumber in secrecy.

Two worlds they have--a globe forgot
  Wheeling from dark to light;
And all the enchanted realm of dream
  That burgeons out of night.

THE STRANGER

Half-hidden in a graveyard,
  In the blackness of a yew,
Where never living creature stirs,
  Nor sunbeam pierces through,

Is a tomb, green and crooked,--
  Its faded legend gone,--
With but one rain-worn cherub's head
  Of smouldering stone.

There, when the dusk is falling,
  Silence broods so deep
It seems that every wind that breathes
  Blows from the field of sleep.

Day breaks in heedless beauty,
  Kindling each drop of dew,
But unforsaking shadow dwells
  Beneath this lonely yew.

And, all else lost and faded,
  Only this listening head
Keeps with a strange unanswering smile
  Its secret with the dead.

NEVER MORE SAILOR

Never more, Sailor,
Shall thou be
Tossed on the wind-ridden,
Restless sea.
Its tides may labour;
All the world
Shake 'neath that weight
Of waters hurled:
But its whole shock
Can only stir
Thy dust to a quiet
Even quieter.
Thou mock'st at land
Who now art come
To such a small
And shallow home;
Yet bore the sea
Full many a care

For bones that once
A sailor's were.
And though the grave's
Deep soundlessness
Thy once sea-deafened
Ear distress,
No robin ever
On the deep
Hopped with his song
To haunt thy sleep.

ARABIA

Far are the shades of Arabia,
  Where the Princes ride at noon,
'Mid the verdurous vales and thickets,
  Under the ghost of the moon;
And so dark is that vaulted purple
  Flowers in the forest rise
And toss into blossom 'gainst the phantom stars
  Pale in the noonday skies.

Sweet is the music of Arabia
  In my heart, when out of dreams
I still in the thin clear mirk of dawn
  Descry her gliding streams;

Hear her strange lutes on the green banks
  Ring loud with the grief and delight
Of the dim-silked dark-haired Musicians
  In the brooding silence of night.

They haunt me--her lutes and her forests;
  No beauty on earth I see
But shadowed with that dreams recalls
  Her loveliness to me:
Still eyes look coldly upon me,
  Cold voices whisper and say--
"He is crazed with the spell of far Arabia,
  They have stolen his wits away."

THE MOUNTAINS

Still, and blanched, and cold, and lone,
  The icy hills far off from me
With frosty ulys overgrown
  Stand in their sculptured secrecy.

No path of theirs the chamois fleet
  Treads, with a nostril to the wind;
O'er their ice-marbled glaciers beat
  No wings of eagles in my mind--

Yea, in my mind these mountains rise,
  Their perils dyed with evening's rose;
And still my ghost sits at my eyes
  And thirsts for their untroubled snows.

QUEEN DJENIRA

When Queen Djenira slumbers through
  The sultry noon's repose,
From out her dreams, as soft she lies,
  A faint thin music flows.

Her lovely hands lie narrow and pale
  With gilded nails, her head
Couched in its handed nets of gold
  Lies pillowed on her bed.

The little Nubian boys who fan
  Her cheeks and tresses clear,
Wonderful, wonderful, wonderful voices
  Seem afar to hear.

They slide their eyes, and nodding, say,
  "Queen Djenira walks to-day
The courts of the lord Pthamasar
  Where the sweet birds of Psuthys are."

And those of earth about her porch
  Of shadow cool and grey
Their sidelong beaks in silence lean,
  And silent flit away.

NEVER-TO-BE

Down by the waters of the sea
Reigns the King of Never-to-be.
His palace walls are black with night;
His torches star and moon's light,
And for his timepiece deep and grave
Beats on the green unhastening wave.

Windswept are his high corridors;
His pleasance the sea-mantled shores;
For sentinel a shadow stands
With hair in heaven, and cloudy hands;
And round his bed, king's guards to be,
Watch pines in iron solemnity.

His hound is mute; his steed at will
Roams pastures deep with asphodel;
His queen is to her slumber gone;
His courtiers mute lie, hewn in stone;

He hath forgot where he did hide
His sceptre in the mountain-side.

Grey-capped and muttering, mad is he--
The childless King of Never-to-be;
For all his people in the deep
Keep, everlasting, fast asleep;
And all his realm is foam and rain,
Whispering of what comes not again.

THE DARK CHATEAU

In dreams a dark chateau
  Stands ever open to me,
In far ravines dream-waters flow,
  Descending soundlessly;
Above its peaks the eagle floats,
  Lone in a sunless sky;
Mute are the golden woodland throats
  Of the birds flitting by.

No voice is audible. The wind
  Sleeps in its peace.
No flower of the light can find
  Refuge beneath its trees;
Only the darkening ivy climbs

Mingled with wilding rose,
And cypress, morn and evening, time's
  Black shadow throws.

All vacant, and unknown;
  Only the dreamer steps
From stone to hollow stone,
  Where the green moss sleeps,
Peers at the rivers in its deeps,
  The eagle lone in the sky,
While the dew of evening drips,
  Coldly and silently.

Would that I could steal in!--
  Into each secret room;
Would that my sleep-bright eyes could win
  To the inner gloom;
Gaze from its high windows,
  Far down its mouldering walls,
Where amber-clear still Lethe flows,
  And foaming falls.

But ever as I gaze,
  From slumber soft doth come
Some touch my stagnant sense to raise
  To its old earthly home;
Fades then that sky serene;
  And peak of ageless snow;
Fades to a paling dawn-lit green,
  My dark chateau.

THE DWELLING-PLACE

Deep in a forest where the kestrel screamed,
  Beside a lake of water, clear as glass,
The time-worn windows of a stone house gleamed
    Named only "Alas."

Yet happy as the wild birds in the glades
  Of that green forest, thridding the still air
With low continued heedless serenades,
    Its heedless people were.

The throbbing chords of violin and lute,
  The lustre of lean tapers in dark eyes,
Fair colours, beauteous flowers, faint-bloomed fruit
    Made earth seem Paradise

To them that dwelt within this lonely house:
  Like children of the gods in lasting peace,
They ate, sang, danced, as if each day's carouse
    Need never pause, nor cease.

Some to the hunt would wend, with hound and horn,
  And clash of silver, beauty, bravery, pride,
Heeding not one who on white horse upborne
    With soundless hoofs did ride.

Dreamers there were who watched the hours away

Beside a fountain's foam. And in the sweet
Of phantom evening, 'neath the night-bird's lay,
    Did loved with loved-one meet.

All, all were children, for, the long day done,
  They barred the heavy door against lightfoot fear;
And few words spake though one known face was gone,
    Yet still seemed hovering near.

They heaped the bright fire higher; poured dark wine;
  And in long revelry dazed the questioning eye;
Curtained three-fold the heart-dismaying shine
    Of midnight streaming by.

They shut the dark out from the painted wall,
  With candles dared the shadow at the door,
Sang down the faint reiterated call
    Of those who came no more.

Yet clear above that portal plain was writ,
  Confronting each at length alone to pass
Out of its beauty into night star-lit,
    That word "Alas!"

THE LISTENERS

"Is there anybody there?" said the Traveller,
  Knocking on the moonlit door;
And his horse in the silence champed the grasses
  Of the forest's ferny floor:
And a bird flew up out of the turret,
  Above the Traveller's head:
And he smote upon the door again a second time;
  "Is there anybody there?" he said.
But no one descended to the Traveller;
  No head from the leaf-fringed sill
Leaned over and looked into his grey eyes,
  Where he stood perplexed and still.
But only a host of phantom listeners
  That dwelt in the lone house then
Stood listening in the quiet of the moonlight
  To that voice from the world of men:
Stood thronging the faint moonbeams on the dark stair,
  That goes down to the empty hall,
Hearkening in an air stirred and shaken
  By the lonely Traveller's call.
And he felt in his heart their strangeness,
  Their stillness answering his cry,
While his horse moved, cropping the dark turf,
  'Neath the starred and leafy sky;
For he suddenly smote on the door, even
  Louder, and lifted his head:--
"Tell them I came, and no one answered,

That I kept my word," he said.
Never the least stir made the listeners,
   Though every word he spake
Fell echoing through the shadowiness of the still house
   From the one man left awake:
Ay, they heard his foot upon the stirrup,
   And the sound of iron on stone,
And how the silence surged softly backward,
   When the plunging hoofs were gone.

TIME PASSES

There was nought in the Valley
   But a Tower of Ivory,
Its base enwreathed with red
   Flowers that at evening
   Caught the sun's crimson
As to Ocean low he sped.

Lucent and lovely
   It stood in the morning
Under a trackless hill;
   With snows eternal
   Muffling its summit,
And silence ineffable.

Sighing of solitude
Winds from the cold heights
Haunted its yellowing stone;
At noon its shadow
Stretched athwart cedars
Whence every bird was flown.

Its stair was broken,
Its starlit walls were
Fretted; its flowers shone
Wide at the portal,
Full-blown and fading,
Their last faint fragrance gone.

And on high in its lantern
A shape of the living
Watched o'er a shoreless sea,
From a Tower rotting
With age and weakness,
Once lovely as ivory.

BEWARE!

An ominous bird sang from its branch,
"Beware, O Wanderer!
Night 'mid her flowers of glamourie spilled

Draws swiftly near:

"Night with her darkened caravans,
  Piled deep with silver and myrrh,
Draws from the portals of the East,
  O Wanderer near."

"Night who walks plumed through the fields
  Of stars that strangely stir--
Smitten to fire by the sandals of him
  Who walks with her."

THE JOURNEY

Heart-sick of his journey was the Wanderer;
  Footsore and parched was he;
And a Witch who long had lurked by the wayside,
  Looked out of sorcery.

"Lift up your eyes, you lonely Wanderer,"
  She peeped from her casement small;
"Here's shelter and quiet to give you rest, young man,
  And apples for thirst withal."

And he looked up out of his sad reverie,
  And saw all the woods in green,

With birds that flitted feathered in the dappling,
  The jewel-bright leaves between.

And he lifted up his face towards her lattice,
  And there, alluring-wise,
Slanting through the silence of the long past,
  Dwelt the still green Witch's eyes.

And vaguely from the hiding-place of memory
  Voices seemed to cry;
"What is the darkness of one brief life-time
  To the deaths thou hast made us die?

"Heed not the words of the Enchantress
  Who would us still betray!"
And sad with the echo of their reproaches,
  Doubting, he turned away.

"I may not shelter beneath your roof, lady,
  Nor in this wood's green shadow seek repose,
Nor will your apples quench the thirst
  A homesick wanderer knows."

"'Homesick' forsooth!" she softly mocked him:
  And the beauty in her face
Made in the sunshine pale and trembling
  A stillness in that place.

And he sighed, as if in fear, that young Wanderer,
  Looking to left and to right,
Where the endless narrow road swept onward,
  Till in distance lost to sight.

And there fell upon his sense the brier,
  Haunting the air with its breath,
And the faint shrill sweetness of the birds' throats,
  Their tent of leaves beneath.

And there was the Witch, in no wise heeding;
  Her arbour, and fruit-filled dish,
Her pitcher of well-water, and clear damask--
  All that the weary wish.

And the last gold beam across the green world
  Faltered and failed, as he
Remembered his solitude and the dark night's
  Inhospitality.

And he looked upon the Witch with eyes of sorrow
  In the darkening of the day;
And turned him aside into oblivion;
  And the voices died away....

And the Witch stepped down from her casement:
  In the hush of night he heard
The calling and wailing in dewy thicket
  Of bird to hidden bird.

And gloom stole all her burning crimson,
  Remote and faint in space
As stars in gathering shadow of the evening
  Seemed now her phantom face.

And one night's rest shall be a myriad,
  Midst dreams that come and go;
Till heedless fate, unmoved by weakness, bring him

This same strange by-way through:

To the beauty of earth that fades in ashes,
  The lips of welcome, and the eyes
More beauteous than the feeble shine of Hesper
  Lone in the lightening skies:

Till once again the Witch's guile entreat him;
  But, worn with wisdom, he
Steadfast and cold shall choose the dark night's
  Inhospitality.

HAUNTED

The rabbit in his burrow keeps
No guarded watch, in peace he sleeps;
The wolf that howls in challenging night
Cowers to her lair at morning light;
The simplest bird entwines a nest
Where she may lean her lovely breast,
Couched in the silence of the bough.
But thou, O man, what rest hast thou?

Thy emptiest solitude can bring
Only a subtler questioning
In thy divided heart. Thy bed

Recalls at dawn what midnight said.
Seek how thou wilt to feign content,
Thy flaming ardour's quickly spent;
Soon thy last company is gone,
And leaves thee--with thyself--alone.

Pomp and great friends may hem thee round,
A thousand busy tasks be found;
Earth's thronging beauties may beguile
Thy longing lovesick heart awhile;
And pride, like clouds of sunset, spread
A changing glory round thy head;
But fade will all; and thou must come,
Hating thy journey, homeless, home.

Rave how thou wilt; unmoved, remote,
That inward presence slumbers not,
Frets out each secret from thy breast,
Gives thee no rally, pause, nor rest,
Scans close thy very thoughts, lest they
Should sap his patient power away,
Answers thy wrath with peace, thy cry
With tenderest taciturnity.

SILENCE

With changeful sound life beats upon the ear;
  Yet, striving for release,
  The most seductive string's

Sweet jargonings,
The happiest throat's
Most easeful, lovely notes
Fall back into a veiling silentness.

Even 'mid the rumour of a moving host,
Blackening the clear green earth,
Vainly 'gainst that thin wall
The trumpets call,
Or with loud hum
The smoke-bemuffled drum:
From that high quietness no reply comes forth.

When, all at peace, two friends at ease alone
Talk out their hearts,--yet still
Between the grace-notes of
The voice of love
From each to each
Trembles a rarer speech,
And with its presence every pause doth fill.

Unmoved it broods, this all-encompassing hush
Of one who stooping near,
No smallest stir will make
Our fear to wake;
But yet intent
Upon some mystery bent
Harkens the lightest word we say, or hear.

WINTER DUSK

Dark frost was in the air without,
  The dusk was still with cold and gloom,
When less than even a shadow came
  And stood within the room.

But of the three around the fire,
  None turned a questioning head to look,
Still read a clear voice, on and on,
  Still stooped they o'er their book.

The children watched their mother's eyes
  Moving on softly line to line;
It seemed to listen too--that shade,
  Yet made no outward sign.

The fire-flames crooned a tiny song,
  No cold wind moved the wintry tree;
The children both in Faerie dreamed
  Beside their mother's knee.

And nearer yet that spirit drew
  Above that heedless one, intent
Only on what the simple words
  Of her small story meant.

No voiceless sorrow grieved her mind,
  No memory her bosom stirred,

Nor dreamed she, as she read to two,
  'Twas surely three who heard.

Yet when, the story done, she smiled
  From face to face, serene and clear,
A love, half dread, sprang up, as she
  Leaned close and drew them near.

THE GHOST

Peace in thy hands,
Peace in thine eyes,
Peace on thy brow;
Flower of a moment in the eternal hour,
Peace with me now.

Not a wave breaks,
Not a bird calls,
My heart, like a sea,
Silent after a storm that hath died,
Sleeps within me.

All the night's dews,
All the world's leaves,
All winter's snow
Seem with their quiet to have stilled in life's dream

All sorrowing now.

AN EPITAPH

Here lies a most beautiful lady,
Light of step and heart was she;
I think she was the most beautiful lady
That ever was in the West Country.
But beauty vanishes; beauty passes;
However rare--rare it be;
And when I crumble, who will remember
This lady of the West Country?

"THE HAWTHORN HATH A DEATHLY SMELL"

The flowers of the field
  Have a sweet smell;
Meadowsweet, tansy, thyme,
  And faint-heart pimpernel;

But sweeter even than these,
  The silver of the may
Wreathed is with incense for
  The Judgment Day.

An apple, a child, dust,
  When falls the evening rain,
Wild brier's spiced leaves,
  Breathe memories again;
With further memory fraught,
  The silver of the may
Wreathed is with incense for
  The Judgment Day.

Eyes of all loveliness--
  Shadow of strange delight,
Even as a flower fades
  Must thou from sight;
But oh, o'er thy grave's mound,
  Till come the Judgment Day,
Wreathed shall with incense he
  Thy sharp-thorned may.

*   *   *   *   *

MOTLEY: 1918

*   *   *   *   *

THE LITTLE SALAMANDER

TO MARGOT

When I go free,
I think 'twill be
A night of stars and snow,
And the wild fires of frost shall light
My footsteps as I go;
Nobody--nobody will be there
With groping touch, or sight,
To see me in my bush of hair
Dance burning through the night.

THE LINNET

Upon this leafy bush
  With thorns and roses in it,
Flutters a thing of light,
  A twittering linnet.
And all the throbbing world
  Of dew and sun and air
By this small parcel of life
  Is made more fair;
As if each bramble-spray
And mounded gold-wreathed furze,
  Harebell and little thyme,
  Were only hers;
As if this beauty and grace
  Did to one bird belong,
And, at a flutter of wing,
  Might vanish in song.

THE SUNKEN GARDEN

Speak not--whisper not;
Here bloweth thyme and bergamot;

Softly on the evening hour,
Secret herbs their spices shower.
Dark-spiked rosemary and myrrh,
Lean-stalked, purple lavender;
Hides within her bosom, too,
All her sorrows, bitter rue.

Breathe not--trespass not;
Of this green and darkling spot,
Latticed from the moon's beams,
Perchance a distant dreamer dreams;
Perchance upon its darkening air,
The unseen ghosts of children fare,
Faintly swinging, sway and sweep,
Like lovely sea-flowers in its deep;
While, unmoved, to watch and ward,
Amid its gloomed and daisied sward,
Stands with bowed and dewy head
That one little leaden Lad.

THE RIDDLERS

"Thou solitary!" the Blackbird cried,
"I, from the happy Wren,
Linnet and Blackcap, Woodlark, Thrush,
Perched all upon a sweetbrier bush,

Have come at cold of midnight-tide
To ask thee, Why and when
Grief smote thy heart so thou dost sing
In solemn hush of evening,
So sorrowfully, lovelorn Thing--
Nay, nay, not sing, but rave, but wail,
Most melancholic Nightingale?
Do not the dews of darkness steep
All pinings of the day in sleep?
Why, then, when rocked in starry nest
We mutely couch, secure, at rest,
Doth thy lone heart delight to make
Music for sorrow's sake?"
A Moon was there. So still her beam,
It seemed the whole world lay in dream,
Lulled by the watery sea.
And from her leafy night-hung nook
Upon this stranger soft did look
The Nightingale: sighed he:--

"'Tis strange, my friend; the Kingfisher
But yestermorn conjured me here
Out of his green and gold to say
Why thou, in splendour of the noon,
Wearest of colour but golden shoon,
And else dost thee array
In a most sombre suit of black?
'Surely,' he sighed, 'some load of grief,
Past all our thinking--and belief--
Must weigh upon his back!'
Do, then, in turn, tell me, If joy
Thy heart as well as voice employ
Why dost thou now most Sable, shine

In plumage woefuller far than mine?
Thy silence is a sadder thing
Than any dirge I sing!"

Thus, then, these two small birds, perched there,
Breathed a strange riddle both did share
Yet neither could expound.
And we--who sing but as we can,
In the small knowledge of a man--
Have we an answer found?
Nay, some are happy whose delight
Is hid even from themselves from sight;
And some win peace who spend
The skill of words to sweeten despair
Of finding consolation where
Life has but one dark end;
Who, in rapt solitude, tell o'er
A tale as lovely as forlore,
Into the midnight air.

MOONLIGHT

The far moon maketh lovers wise
  In her pale beauty trembling down,
Lending curved cheeks, dark lips, dark eyes,
  A strangeness not her own.

And, though they shut their lids to kiss,
  In starless darkness peace to win,
Even on that secret world from this
  Her twilight enters in.

THE BLIND BOY

"I have no master," said the Blind Boy,
  "My mother, 'Dame Venus' they do call;
Cowled in this hood she sent me begging
  For whate'er in pity may befall.

"Hard was her visage, me adjuring,--
  'Have no fond mercy on the kind!
Here be sharp arrows, bunched in quiver,
  Draw close ere striking--thou art blind.'

"So stand I here, my woes entreating,
  In this dark alley, lest the Moon
Point with her sparkling my barbed armoury
  Shine on my silver-laced shoon.

"Oh, sir, unkind this Dame to me-ward;
  Of the salt billow was her birth ...
In your sweet charity draw nearer
  The saddest rogue on Earth!"

THE QUARRY

You hunted me with all the pack,
  Too blind, too blind, to see
By no wild hope of force or greed
  Could you make sure of me.

And like a phantom through the glades,
  With tender breast aglow,
The goddess in me laughed to hear
  Your horns a-roving go.

She laughed to think no mortal ever
  By dint of mortal flesh
The very Cause that was the Hunt
  One moment could enmesh:

That though with captive limbs I lay,
  Stilled breath and vanquished eyes,
He that hunts Love with horse and hound
  Hunts out his heart and eyes.

MRS. GRUNDY

"Step very softly, sweet Quiet-foot,
Stumble not, whisper not, smile not:
By this dark ivy stoop cheek and brow.
Still even thy heart! What seest thou?..."

"High-coifed, broad-browed, aged, suave yet grim,
A large flat face, eyes keenly dim,
Staring at nothing--that's me!--and yet,
With a hate one could never, no, never forget ..."

"This is my world, my garden, my home,
Hither my father bade mother to come
And bear me out of the dark into light,
And happy I was in her tender sight.

"And then, thou frail flower, she died and went,
Forgetting my pitiless banishment,
And that Old Woman--an Aunt--she said,
Came hither, lodged, fattened, and made her bed.

"Oh yes, thou most blessed, from Monday to Sunday,
Has lived on me, preyed on me, Mrs. Grundy:
Called me, 'dear Nephew'; on each of those chairs
Has gloated in righteousness, heard my prayers.

"Why didst thou dare the thorns of the grove,
Timidest trespasser, huntress of love?

Now thou hast peeped, and now dost know
What kind of creature is thine for foe.

"Not that she'll tear out thy innocent eyes,
Poison thy mouth with deviltries.
Watch thou, wait thou: soon will begin
The guile of a voice: hark!..." "Come in, Come in!"

THE TRYST

Flee into some forgotten night and be
Of all dark long my moon-bright company:
Beyond the rumour even of Paradise come,
There, out of all remembrance, make our home:
Seek we some close hid shadow for our lair,
Hollowed by Noah's mouse beneath the chair
Wherein the Omnipotent, in slumber bound,
Nods till the piteous Trump of Judgment sound.
Perchance Leviathan of the deep sea
Would lease a lost mermaiden's grot to me,
There of your beauty we would joyance make--
A music wistful for the sea-nymph's sake:
Haply Elijah, o'er his spokes of fire,
Cresting steep Leo, or the heavenly Lyre,
Spied, tranced in azure of inanest space,
Some eyrie hostel, meet for human grace,

Where two might happy be--just you and I--
Lost in the uttermost of Eternity.
Think! In Time's smallest clock's minutest beat
Might there not rest be found for wandering feet?
Or, 'twixt the sleep and wake of Helen's dream,
Silence wherein to sing love's requiem?
No, no. Nor earth, nor air, nor fire, nor deep
Could lull poor mortal longingness asleep.
Somewhere there Nothing is; and there lost Man
Shall win what changeless vague of peace he can.

ALONE

The abode of the nightingale is bare,
Flowered frost congeals in the gelid air,
The fox howls from his frozen lair:
    Alas, my loved one is gone,
    I am alone:
    It is winter.

Once the pink cast a winy smell,
The wild bee hung in the hyacinth bell,
Light in effulgence of beauty fell:
    Alas, my loved one is gone,
    I am alone:
    It is winter.

My candle a silent fire doth shed,
Starry Orion hunts o'erhead;
Come moth, come shadow, the world is dead:
    Alas, my loved one is gone,
    I am alone:
    It is winter.

THE EMPTY HOUSE

See this house, how dark it is
Beneath its vast-boughed trees!
Not one trembling leaflet cries
To that Watcher in the skies--
"Remove, remove thy searching gaze,
Innocent, of heaven's ways,
Brood not, Moon, so wildly bright,
On secrets hidden from sight."

"Secrets," sighs the night-wind,
"Vacancy is all I find;
Every keyhole I have made
Wails a summons, faint and sad,
No voice ever answers me,
    Only vacancy."
"Once, once ..." the cricket shrills,

And far and near the quiet fills
With its tiny voice, and then
    Hush falls again.

Mute shadows creeping slow
Mark how the hours go.
Every stone is mouldering slow.
And the least winds that blow
Some minutest atom shake,
Some fretting ruin make
In roof and walls. How black it is
Beneath these thick-boughed trees!

MISTRESS FELL

"Whom seek you here, sweet Mistress Fell?"
"One who loved me passing well.
Dark his eye, wild his face--
Stranger, if in this lonely place
Bide such an one, then, prythee, say
I am come here to-day."

"Many his like, Mistress Fell?"
"I did not look, so cannot tell.
Only this I surely know,
When his voice called me, I must go;

Touched me his fingers, and my heart
Leapt at the sweet pain's smart."

"Why did he leave you, Mistress Fell?"
"Magic laid its dreary spell.--
Stranger, he was fast asleep;
Into his dream I tried to creep;
Called his name, soft was my cry;
He answered--not one sigh.

"The flower and the thorn are here;
Falleth the night-dew, cold and clear;
Out of her bower the bird replies,
Mocking the dark with ecstasies,
See how the earth's green grass doth grow,
Praising what sleeps below!

"Thus have they told me. And I come,
As flies the wounded wild-bird home.
Not tears I give; but all that he
Clasped in his arms, sweet charity;
All that he loved--to him I bring
For a close whispering."

THE GHOST

"Who knocks?" "I, who was beautiful,
  Beyond all dreams to restore,
I, from the roots of the dark thorn am hither.

And knock on the door."

"Who speaks?" "I--once was my speech
  Sweet as the bird's on the air,
When echo lurks by the waters to heed;
  'Tis I speak thee fair."

"Dark is the hour!" "Ay, and cold."
  "Lone is my house." "Ah, but mine?"
"Sight, touch, lips, eyes yearned in vain."
  "Long dead these to thine ..."

Silence. Still faint on the porch
  Brake the flames of the stars.
In gloom groped a hope-wearied hand
  Over keys, bolts, and bars.

A face peered. All the grey night
  In chaos of vacancy shone;
Nought but vast sorrow was there--
  The sweet cheat gone.

THE STRANGER

In the woods as I did walk,
  Dappled with the moon's beam,

I did with a Stranger talk,
  And his name was Dream.

Spurred his heel, dark his cloak,
  Shady-wide his bonnet's brim;
His horse beneath a silvery oak
  Grazed as I talked with him.

Softly his breast-brooch burned and shone;
  Hill and deep were in his eyes;
One of his hands held mine, and one
  The fruit that makes men wise.

Wondrously strange was earth to see,
  Flowers white as milk did gleam;
Spread to Heaven the Assyrian Tree,
  Over my head with Dream.

Dews were still betwixt us twain;
  Stars a trembling beauty shed;
Yet--not a whisper comes again
  Of the words he said.

BETRAYAL

She will not die, they say,

She will but put her beauty by
    And hie away.

Oh, but her beauty gone, how lonely
Then will seem all reverie,
    How black to me!

All things will sad be made
And every hope a memory,
    All gladness dead.

Ghosts of the past will know
My weakest hour, and whisper to me,
    And coldly go.

And hers in deep of sleep,
Clothed in its mortal beauty I shall see,
    And, waking, weep.

Naught will my mind then find
In man's false Heaven my peace to be:
    All blind, and blind.

THE CAGE

Why did you flutter in vain hope, poor bird,

Hard-pressed in your small cage of clay?
'Twas but a sweet, false echo that you heard,
   Caught only a feint of day.

Still is the night all dark, a homeless dark.
  Burn yet the unanswering stars. And silence brings
The same sea's desolate surge--sans bound or mark--
   Of all your wanderings.

Fret now no more; be still. Those steadfast eyes,
  Those folded hands, they cannot set you free;
Only with beauty wake wild memories--
  Sorrow for where you are, for where you would be.

THE REVENANT

O all ye fair ladies with your colours and your graces,
  And your eyes clear in flame of candle and hearth,
Toward the dark of this old window lift not up your smiling faces,
  Where a Shade stands forlorn from the cold of the earth.

God knows I could not rest for one I still was thinking of;
  Like a rose sheathed in beauty her spirit was to me;
Now out of unforgottenness a bitter draught I'm drinking of,
  'Tis sad of such beauty unremembered to be.

Men all all shades, O Woman.--Winds wist not of the way they blow.
  Apart from your kindness, life's at best but a snare.
Though a tongue now past praise this bitter thing doth say, I know
  What solitude means, and how, homeless, I fare.

Strange, strange, are ye all--except in beauty shared with her--
  Since I seek one I loved, yet was faithless to in death.
Not life enough I heaped, so thus my heart must fare with her,
  Now wrapt in the gross clay, bereft of life's breath.

MUSIC

When music sounds, gone is the earth I know,
And all her lovely things even lovelier grow;
Her flowers in vision flame, her forest trees,
Lift burdened branches, stilled with ecstasies.

When music sounds, out of the water rise
Naiads whose beauty dims my waking eyes,
Rapt in strange dreams burns each enchanted face,
With solemn echoing stirs their dwelling-place.

When music sounds, all that I was I am
Ere to this haunt of brooding dust I came;
While from Time's woods break into distant song
The swift-winged hours, as I hasten along.

THE REMONSTRANCE

I was at peace until you came
And set a careless mind aflame.
I lived in quiet; cold, content;
All longing in safe banishment,
Until your ghostly lips and eyes
   Made wisdom unwise.

Naught was in me to tempt your feet
To seek a lodging. Quite forgot
Lay the sweet solitude we two
In childhood used to wander through;
Time's cold had closed my heart about;
   And shut you out.

Well, and what then?... O vision grave,
Take all the little all I have!
Strip me of what in voiceless thought
Life's kept of life, unhoped, unsought!--
Reverie and dream that memory must
   Hide deep in dust!

This only I say:--Though cold and bare
The haunted house you have chosen to share,

Still 'neath its walls the moonbeam goes
   And trembles on the untended rose;

Still o'er its broken roof-tree rise
The starry arches of the skies;
And in your lightest word shall be
   The thunder of an ebbing sea.

NOCTURNE

'Tis not my voice now speaks; but a bird
In darkling forest hollows a sweet throat--
Pleads on till distant echo too hath heard
   And doubles every note:
So love that shrouded dwells in mystery
   Would cry and waken thee.

Thou Solitary, stir in thy still sleep;
All the night waits thee, yet thou still dream'st on.
Furtive the shadows that about thee creep,
And cheat the shining footsteps of the moon:
Unseal thine eyes, it is my heart that sings,
   And beats in vain its wings.

Lost in heaven's vague, the stars burn softly through
The world's dark latticings, we prisoned stray

Within its lovely labyrinth, and know
   Mute seraphs guard the way
Even from silence unto speech, from love
To that self's self it still is dreaming of.

THE EXILE

I am that Adam who, with Snake for guest,
Hid anguished eyes upon Eve's piteous breast.
I am that Adam who, with broken wings,
Fled from the Seraph's brazen trumpetings.
Betrayed and fugitive, I still must roam
A world where sin, and beauty, whisper of Home.

Oh, from wide circuit, shall at length I see
Pure daybreak lighten again on Eden's tree?
Loosed from remorse and hope and love's distress,
Enrobe me again in my lost nakedness?
No more with wordless grief a loved one grieve,
But to Heaven's nothingness re-welcome Eve?

THE UNCHANGING

After the songless rose of evening,
    Night quiet, dark, still,
In nodding cavalcade advancing
    Starred the deep hill:
You, in the valley standing,
    In your quiet wonder took
All that glamour, peace, and mystery
    In one grave look.
Beauty hid your naked body,
    Time dreamed in your bright hair,
In your eyes the constellations
    Burned far and fair.

INVOCATION

The burning fire shakes in the night,
    On high her silver candles gleam,
With far-flung arms enflamed with light,
    The trees are lost in dream.

Come in thy beauty! 'tis my love,
　Lost in far-wandering desire,
Hath in the darkling deep above
　Set stars and kindled fire.

EYES

O strange devices that alone divide
The seer from the seen--
The very highway of earth's pomp and pride
That lies between
The traveller and the cheating, sweet delight
Of where he longs to be,
But which, bound hand and foot, he, close on night,
Can only see.

LIFE

Hearken, O dear, now strikes the hour we die;

We, who in our strange kiss
Have proved a dream the world's realities,
Turned each from other's darkness with a sigh,
Need heed no more of life, waste no more breath
On any other journey, but of death.

And yet: Oh, know we well
How each of us must prove Love's infidel;
Still out of ecstasy turn trembling back
To earth's same empty track
Of leaden day by day, and hour by hour, and be
Of all things lovely the cold mortuary.

THE DISGUISE

Why in my heart, O Grief,
Dost thou in beauty hide?
Dead is my well-content,
And buried deep my pride.
Cold are their stones, beloved,
To hand and side.

The shadows of even are gone,
Shut are the day's clear flowers,
Now have her birds left mute
Their singing bowers,

Lone shall we be, we twain,
In the night hours.

Thou with thy cheek on mine,
And dark hair loosed, shall see
Take the far stars for fruit
The cypress tree,
And in the yew's black
Shall the moon be.

We will tell no old tales,
Nor heed if in wandering air
Die a lost song of love
Or the once fair;
Still as well-water be
The thoughts we share!

And, while the ghosts keep
Tryst from chill sepulchres,
Dreamless our gaze shall sleep,
And sealed our ears;
Heart unto heart will speak,
Without tears.

O, thy veiled, lovely face--
Joy's strange disguise--
Shall be the last to fade
From these rapt eyes,
Ere the first dart of daybreak
Pierce the skies.

VAIN QUESTIONING

What needest thou?--a few brief hours of rest
Wherein to seek thyself in thine own breast;
A transient silence wherein truth could say
Such was thy constant hope, and this thy way?--
    O burden of life that is
    A livelong tangle of perplexities!

What seekest thou?--a truce from that thou art;
Some steadfast refuge from a fickle heart;
Still to be thou, and yet no thing of scorn,
To find no stay here, and yet not forlorn?--
    O riddle of life that is
    An endless war 'twixt contrarieties.

Leave this vain questioning. Is not sweet the rose?
Sings not the wild bird ere to rest he goes?
Hath not in miracle brave June returned?
Burns not her beauty as of old it burned?
    O foolish one to roam
    So far in thine own mind away from home!

Where blooms the flower when her petals fade,
Where sleepeth echo by earth's music made,
Where all things transient to the changeless win,
There waits the peace thy spirit dwelleth in.

VIGIL

Dark is the night,
  The fire burns faint and low,
Hours--days--years,
  Into grey ashes go;
I strive to read,
  But sombre is the glow.

Thumbed are the pages,
  And the print is small;
Mocking the winds
  That from the darkness call;
Feeble the fire that lends
  Its light withal.

O ghost, draw nearer;
  Let thy shadowy hair,
Blot out the pages
  That we cannot share;
Be ours the one last leaf
  By Fate left bare!

Let's Finis scrawl,
  And then Life's book put by;
Turn each to each

In all simplicity:
Ere the last flame is gone
  To warm us by.

THE OLD MEN

Old and alone, sit we,
  Caged, riddle-rid men;
Lost to Earth's "Listen!" and "See!"
  Thought's "Wherefore?" and "When?"

Only far memories stray
  Of a past once lovely, but now
Wasted and faded away,
  Like green leaves from the bough.

Vast broods the silence of night,
  The ruinous moon
Lifts on our faces her light,
  Whence all dreaming is gone.

We speak not; trembles each head;
  In their sockets our eyes are still;
Desire as cold as the dead;
  Without wonder or will.
And One, with a lanthorn, draws near,

At clash with the moon in our eyes:
"Where art thou?" he asks: "I am here,"
  One by one we arise.

And none lifts a hand to withhold
  A friend from the touch of that foe:
Heart cries unto heart, "Thou art old!"
  Yet, reluctant, we go.

THE DREAMER

O thou who giving helm and sword,
  Gav'st, too, the rusting rain,
And starry dark's all tender dews
    To blunt and stain:

Out of the battle I am sped,
  Unharmed, yet stricken sore;
A living shape amid whispering shades
    On Lethe's shore.

No trophy in my hands I bring,
  To this sad, sighing stream,
The neighings and the trumps and cries
    Were but a dream.

Traitor to life, of life betrayed:
  O, of thy mercy deep,
A dream my all, the all I ask
    Is sleep.

MOTLEY

Come, Death, I'd have a word with thee;
And thou, poor Innocency;
And love--a Lad with broken wing;
And Pity, too:
The Fool shall sing to you,
As Fools will sing.

Ay, music hath small sense,
And a tune's soon told,
And Earth is old,
And my poor wits are dense;
Yet have I secrets,--dark, my dear,
To breathe you all: Come near.
And lest some hideous listener tells,
I'll ring my bells.

They are all at war!--
Yes, yes, their bodies go
'Neath burning sun and icy star

To chaunted songs of woe,
Dragging cold cannon through a mire
Of rain and blood and spouting fire,
The new moon glinting hard on eyes
Wide with insanities!

Hush!... I use words
I hardly know the meaning of;
And the mute birds
Are glancing at Love
From out their shade of leaf and flower,
Trembling at treacheries
Which even in noonday cower.
Heed, heed not what I said
Of frenzied hosts of men,
More fools than I,
On envy, hatred fed,
Who kill, and die--
Spake I not plainly, then?
Yet Pity whispered, "Why?"

Thou silly thing, off to thy daisies go.
Mine was not news for child to know,
And Death--no ears hath. He hath supped where creep
Eyeless worms in hush of sleep;
Yet, when he smiles, the hand he draws
Athwart his grinning jaws--
Faintly the thin bones rattle, and--There, there;
Hearken how my bells in the air
Drive away care!...

Nay, but a dream I had
Of a world all mad.

Not simply happy mad like me,
Who am mad like an empty scene
Of water and willow tree,
Where the wind hath been;
But that foul Satan-mad,
Who rots in his own head,
And counts the dead,
Not honest one--and two--
But for the ghosts they were,
Brave, faithful, true,
When, head in air,
In Earth's clear green and blue
Heaven they did share
With beauty who bade them there ...
There, now! Death goes--
Mayhap I've wearied him.
Ay, and the light doth dim,
And asleep's the rose,
And tired Innocence
In dreams is hence ...
Come, Love, my lad,
Nodding that drowsy head,
'Tis time thy prayers were said!

THE MARIONETTES

Let the foul Scene proceed:
  There's laughter in the wings;
'Tis sawdust that they bleed,
  But a box Death brings.

How rare a skill is theirs
  These extreme pangs to show,
How real a frenzy wears
  Each feigner of woe!

Gigantic dins uprise!
  Even the gods must feel
A smarting of the eyes
  As these fumes upsweal.

Strange, such a Piece is free,
  While we Spectators sit,
Aghast at its agony,
  Yet absorbed in it!

Dark is the outer air,
  Cold the night draughts blow
Mutely we stare, and stare
  At the frenzied Show.

Yet heaven hath its quiet shroud
  Of deep, immutable blue--

We cry "An end!" We are bowed
  By the dread, "'Tis true!"

While the Shape who hoofs applause
  Behind our deafened ear,
Hoots--angel-wise--"the Cause!"
  And affright even fear.

TO E.T.: 1917

You sleep too well--too far away,
  For sorrowing word to soothe or wound;
Your very quiet seems to say
  How longed-for a peace you have found.

Else, had not death so lured you on,
  You would have grieved--'twixt joy and fear--
To know how my small loving son
  Had wept for you, my dear.

APRIL MOON

Roses are sweet to smell and see,
  And lilies on the stem;
But rarer, stranger buds there be,
  And she was like to them.

The little moon that April brings,
  More lovely shade than light,
That, setting, silvers lonely hills
  Upon the verge of night--

Close to the world of my poor heart
  So stole she, still and clear;
Now that she's gone, O dark, and dark,
  The solitude, the fear.

THE FOOL'S SONG

Never, no never, listen too long,
To the chattering wind in the willow, the night bird's song.

'Tis sad in sooth to lie under the grass,

But none too gladsome to wake and grow cold where life's shadows pass.

Dumb the old Toll-Woman squats,
And, for every green copper battered and worn, doles out Nevers and Nots.

I know a Blind Man, too,
Who with a sharp ear listens and listens the whole world through.

Oh, sit we snug to our feast,
With platter and finger and spoon--and good victuals at least.

CLEAR EYES

Clear eyes do dim at last,
  And cheeks outlive their rose.
Time, heedless of the past,
  No loving-kindness knows;
Chill unto mortal lip
  Still Lethe flows.

Griefs, too, but brief while stay,
  And sorrow, being o'er,
Its salt tears shed away,
  Woundeth the heart no more.
Stealthily lave those waters
  That solemn shore.

Ah, then, sweet face burn on,
  While yet quick memory lives!
And Sorrow, ere thou art gone,
  Know that my heart forgives--
Ere yet, grown cold in peace,
  It loves not, nor grieves.

DUST TO DUST

Heavenly Archer, bend thy bow;
Now the flame of life burns low,
Youth is gone; I, too, would go.

Even Fortune leads to this:
Harsh or kind, at last she is
Murderess of all ecstasies.

Yet the spirit, dark, alone,
Bound in sense, still hearkens on
For tidings of a bliss foregone.

Sleep is well for dreamless head,
At no breath astonished,
From the Gardens of the Dead.

I the immortal harps hear ring,
By Babylon's river languishing.
Heavenly Archer, loose thy string.

THE THREE STRANGERS

Far are those tranquil hills,
  Dyed with fair evening's rose;
On urgent, secret errand bent,
  A traveller goes.

Approach him strangers three,
  Barefooted, cowled; their eyes
Scan the lone, hastening solitary
  With dumb surmise.

One instant in close speech
  With them he doth confer:
God-sped, he hasteneth on,
  That anxious traveller ...

I was that man--in a dream:
  And each world's night in vain
I patient wait on sleep to unveil
  Those vivid hills again.

Would that they three could know
  How yet burns on in me
Love--from one lost in Paradise--
  For their grave courtesy.

ALEXANDER

It was the Great Alexander,
  Capped with a golden helm,
Sate in the ages, in his floating ship,
  In a dead calm.

Voices of sea-maids singing
  Wandered across the deep:
The sailors labouring on their oars
  Rowed, as in sleep.

All the high pomp of Asia,
  Charmed by that siren lay,
Out of their weary and dreaming minds,
  Faded away.

Like a bold boy sate their Captain,
  His glamour withered and gone,
In the souls of his brooding mariners,
  While the song pined on.

Time, like a falling dew,
  Life, like the scene of a dream,
Laid between slumber and slumber,
    Only did seem....

O Alexander, then,
  In all us mortals too,
Wax thou not bold--too bold
    On the wave dark-blue!

Come the calm, infinite night,
  Who then will hear
Aught save the singing
    Of the sea-maids clear?

THE REAWAKENING

Green in light are the hills, and a calm wind flowing
  Filleth the void with a flood of the fragrance of Spring;
Wings in this mansion of life are coming and going,
  Voices of unseen loveliness carol and sing.

Coloured with buds of delight the boughs are swaying,
  Beauty walks in the woods, and wherever she rove
Flowers from wintry sleep, her enchantment obeying,

Stir in the deep of her dream, reawaken to love.

Oh, now begone sullen care--this light is my seeing;
  I am the palace, and mine are its windows and walls;
Daybreak is come, and life from the darkness of being
  Springs, like a child from the womb, when the lonely one calls.

THE VACANT DAY

As I did walk in meadows green
  I heard the summer noon resound
With call of myriad things unseen
  That leapt and crept upon the ground.

High overhead the windless air
  Throbbed with the homesick coursing cry
Of swallows that did everywhere
  Wake echo in the sky.

Beside me, too, clear waters coursed
  Which willow branches, lapsing low,
Breaking their crystal gliding forced
  To sing as they did flow.

I listened; and my heart was dumb
  With praise no language could express;

Longing in vain for him to come
  Who had breathed such blessedness

On this fair world, wherein we pass
  So chequered and so brief a stay;
And yearned in spirit to learn, alas,
  What kept him still away.

THE FLIGHT

How do the days press on, and lay
  Their fallen locks at evening down,
Whileas the stars in darkness play
  And moonbeams weave a crown--

A crown of flower-like light in heaven,
  Where in the hollow arch of space
Morn's mistress dreams, and the Pleiads seven
  Stand watch about her place.

Stand watch--O days no number keep
  Of hours when this dark clay is blind.
When the world's clocks are dumb in sleep
  'Tis then I seek my kind.

FOR ALL THE GRIEF

For all the grief I have given with words
  May now a few clear flowers blow,
In the dust, and the heat, and the silence of birds,
    Where the lonely go.

For the thing unsaid that heart asked of me
  Be a dark, cool water calling--calling
To the footsore, benighted, solitary,
    When the shadows are falling.

O, be beauty for all my blindness,
  A moon in the air where the weary wend,
And dews burdened with loving-kindness
    In the dark of the end.

THE SCRIBE

What lovely things

Thy hand hath made:
The smooth-plumed bird
  In its emerald shade,
The seed of the grass,
  The speck of stone
Which the wayfaring ant
  Stirs--and hastes on!

Though I should sit
  By some tarn in thy hills,
Using its ink
  As the spirit wills
To write of Earth's wonders,
  Its live, willed things,
Flit would the ages
  On soundless wings.
Ere unto Z
  My pen drew nigh;
Leviathan told,
  And the honey-fly:
And still would remain
  My wit to try
My worn reeds broken,
  The dark tarn dry,
All words forgotten--
  Thou, Lord, and I.

FARE WELL

When I lie where shades of darkness
Shall no more assail mine eyes,
Nor the rain make lamentation
    When the wind sighs;
How will fare the world whose wonder
Was the very proof of me?
Memory fades, must the remembered
    Perishing be?

Oh, when this my dust surrenders
Hand, foot, lip, to dust again,
May these loved and loving faces
    Please other men!
May the rustling harvest hedgerow
Still the Traveller's Joy entwine,
And as happy children gather
    Posies once mine.

Look thy last on all things lovely,
Every hour. Let no night
Seal thy sense in deathly slumber
    Till to delight
Thou have paid thy utmost blessing;
Since that all things thou wouldst praise
Beauty took from those who loved them
    In other days.

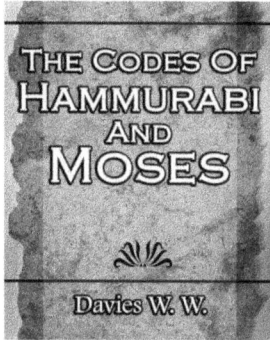

The Codes Of Hammurabi And Moses
W. W. Davies

QTY

The discovery of the Hammurabi Code is one of the greatest achievements of archaeology, and is of paramount interest, not only to the student of the Bible, but also to all those interested in ancient history...

Religion   ISBN: *1-59462-338-4*   **Pages:132**
MSRP $12.95

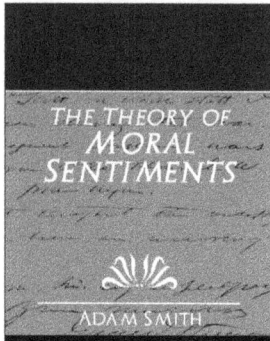

The Theory of Moral Sentiments
Adam Smith

QTY

This work from 1749. contains original theories of conscience amd moral judgment and it is the foundation for systemof morals.

Philosophy ISBN: *1-59462-777-0*   **Pages:536**
MSRP $19.95

Jessica's First Prayer
Hesba Stretton

QTY

In a screened and secluded corner of one of the many railway-bridges which span the streets of London there could be seen a few years ago, from five o'clock every morning until half past eight, a tidily set-out coffee-stall, consisting of a trestle and board, upon which stood two large tin cans, with a small fire of charcoal burning under each so as to keep the coffee boiling during the early hours of the morning when the work-people were thronging into the city on their way to their daily toil...

Pages:84

Childrens   ISBN: *1-59462-373-2*   *MSRP $9.95*

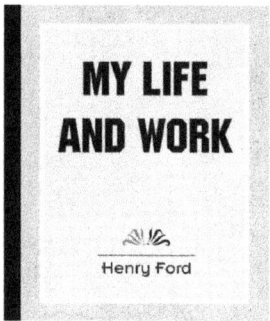

My Life and Work
Henry Ford

QTY

Henry Ford revolutionized the world with his implementation of mass production for the Model T automobile. Gain valuable business insight into his life and work with his own auto-biography... "We have only started on our development of our country we have not as yet, with all our talk of wonderful progress, done more than scratch the surface. The progress has been wonderful enough but..."

Pages:300

Biographies/   ISBN: *1-59462-198-5*   *MSRP $21.95*

www.bookjungle.com *email: sales@bookjungle.com fax: 630-214-0564 mail: Book Jungle PO Box 2226 Champaign, IL 61825*

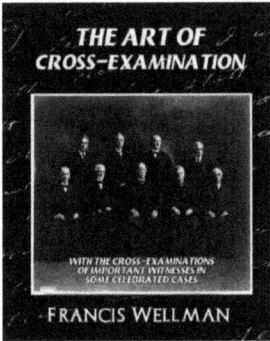

The Art of Cross-Examination
Francis Wellman

QTY

I presume it is the experience of every author, after his first book is published upon an important subject, to be almost overwhelmed with a wealth of ideas and illustrations which could readily have been included in his book, and which to his own mind, at least, seem to make a second edition inevitable. Such certainly was the case with me; and when the first edition had reached its sixth impression in five months, I rejoiced to learn that it seemed to my publishers that the book had met with a sufficiently favorable reception to justify a second and considerably enlarged edition. ...

Pages:412

Reference   ISBN: *1-59462-647-2*   *MSRP $19.95*

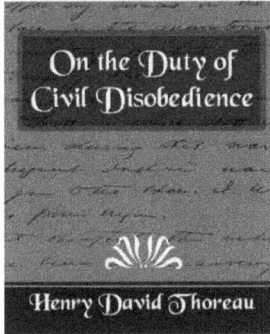

On the Duty of Civil Disobedience
Henry David Thoreau

QTY

Thoreau wrote his famous essay, On the Duty of Civil Disobedience, as a protest against an unjust but popular war and the immoral but popular institution of slave-owning. He did more than write—he declined to pay his taxes, and was hauled off to gaol in consequence. Who can say how much this refusal of his hastened the end of the war and of slavery ?

Law   ISBN: *1-59462-747-9*   **Pages:48**
MSRP $7.45

Dream Psychology Psychoanalysis for Beginners
Sigmund Freud

QTY

Sigmund Freud, born Sigismund Schlomo Freud (May 6, 1856 - September 23, 1939), was a Jewish-Austrian neurologist and psychiatrist who co-founded the psychoanalytic school of psychology. Freud is best known for his theories of the unconscious mind, especially involving the mechanism of repression; his redefinition of sexual desire as mobile and directed towards a wide variety of objects; and his therapeutic techniques, especially his understanding of transference in the therapeutic relationship and the presumed value of dreams as sources of insight into unconscious desires.

Pages:196

Psychology   ISBN: *1-59462-905-6*   *MSRP $15.45*

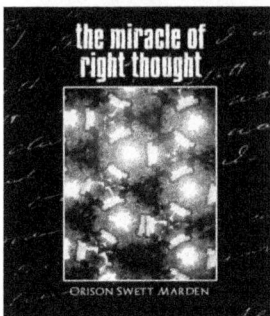

The Miracle of Right Thought
Orison Swett Marden

QTY

Believe with all of your heart that you will do what you were made to do. When the mind has once formed the habit of holding cheerful, happy, prosperous pictures, it will not be easy to form the opposite habit. It does not matter how improbable or how far away this realization may see, or how dark the prospects may be, if we visualize them as best we can, as vividly as possible, hold tenaciously to them and vigorously struggle to attain them, they will gradually become actualized, realized in the life. But a desire, a longing without endeavor, a yearning abandoned or held indifferently will vanish without realization.

Pages:360

Self Help   ISBN: *1-59462-644-8*   *MSRP $25.45*

www.**bookjungle**.com *email: sales@bookjungle.com fax: 630-214-0564 mail: Book Jungle PO Box 2226 Champaign, IL 61825*

QTY

The Rosicrucian Cosmo-Conception Mystic Christianity by *Max Heindel*   ISBN: *1-59462-188-8* **$38.95**
The Rosicrucian Cosmo-conception is not dogmatic, neither does it appeal to any other authority than the reason of the student. It is: not controversial, but is: sent forth in the, hope that it may help to clear...   New Age/Religion Pages 646

Abandonment To Divine Providence by *Jean-Pierre de Caussade*   ISBN: *1-59462-228-0* **$25.95**
"The Rev. Jean Pierre de Caussade was one of the most remarkable spiritual writers of the Society of Jesus in France in the 18th Century. His death took place at Toulouse in 1751. His works have gone through many editions and have been republished...   Inspirational/Religion Pages 400

Mental Chemistry by *Charles Haanel*   ISBN: *1-59462-192-6* **$23.95**
Mental Chemistry allows the change of material conditions by combining and appropriately utilizing the power of the mind. Much like applied chemistry creates something new and unique out of careful combinations of chemicals the mastery of mental chemistry...   New Age Pages 354

The Letters of Robert Browning and Elizabeth Barret Barrett 1845-1846 vol II   ISBN: *1-59462-193-4* **$35.95**
by *Robert Browning* and *Elizabeth Barrett*   Biographies Pages 596

Gleanings In Genesis (volume I) by *Arthur W. Pink*   ISBN: *1-59462-130-6* **$27.45**
Appropriately has Genesis been termed "the seed plot of the Bible" for in it we have, in germ form, almost all of the great doctrines which are afterwards fully developed in the books of Scripture which follow...   Religion/Inspirational Pages 420

The Master Key by *L. W. de Laurence*   ISBN: *1-59462-001-6* **$30.95**
In no branch of human knowledge has there been a more lively increase of the spirit of research during the past few years than in the study of Psychology, Concentration and Mental Discipline. The requests for authentic lessons in Thought Control, Mental Discipline and...   New Age/Business Pages 422

The Lesser Key Of Solomon Goetia by *L. W. de Laurence*   ISBN: *1-59462-092-X* **$9.95**
This translation of the first book of the "Lemegton" which is now for the first time made accessible to students of Talismanic Magic was done, after careful collation and edition, from numerous Ancient Manuscripts in Hebrew, Latin, and French...   New Age/Occult Pages 92

Rubaiyat Of Omar Khayyam by *Edward Fitzgerald*   ISBN:*1-59462-332-5* **$13.95**
Edward Fitzgerald, whom the world has already learned, in spite of his own efforts to remain within the shadow of anonymity, to look upon as one of the rarest poets of the century, was born at Bredfield, in Suffolk, on the 31st of March, 1809. He was the third son of John Purcell...   Music Pages 172

Ancient Law by *Henry Maine*   ISBN: *1-59462-128-4* **$29.95**
The chief object of the following pages is to indicate some of the earliest ideas of mankind, as they are reflected in Ancient Law, and to point out the relation of those ideas to modern thought.   Religiom/History Pages 452

Far-Away Stories by *William J. Locke*   ISBN: *1-59462-129-2* **$19.45**
"Good wine needs no bush, but a collection of mixed vintages does. And this book is just such a collection. Some of the stories I do not want to remain buried for ever in the museum files of dead magazine-numbers an author's not unpardonable vanity..."   Fiction Pages 272

Life of David Crockett by *David Crockett*   ISBN: *1-59462-250-7* **$27.45**
"Colonel David Crockett was one of the most remarkable men of the times in which he lived. Born in humble life, but gifted with a strong will, an indomitable courage, and unremitting perseverance...   Biographies/New Age Pages 424

Lip-Reading by *Edward Nitchie*   ISBN: *1-59462-206-X* **$25.95**
Edward B. Nitchie, founder of the New York School for the Hard of Hearing, now the Nitchie School of Lip-Reading, Inc, wrote "LIP-READING Principles and Practice". The development and perfecting of this meritorious work on lip-reading was an undertaking...   How-to Pages 400

A Handbook of Suggestive Therapeutics, Applied Hypnotism, Psychic Science   ISBN: *1-59462-214-0* **$24.95**
by *Henry Munro*   Health/New Age/Health/Self-help Pages 376

A Doll's House: and Two Other Plays by *Henrik Ibsen*   ISBN: *1-59462-112-8* **$19.95**
Henrik Ibsen created this classic when in revolutionary 1848 Rome. Introducing some striking concepts in playwriting for the realist genre, this play has been studied the world over.   Fiction/Classics/Plays 308

The Light of Asia by *sir Edwin Arnold*   ISBN: *1-59462-204-3* **$13.95**
In this poetic masterpiece, Edwin Arnold describes the life and teachings of Buddha. The man who was to become known as Buddha to the world was born as Prince Gautama of India but he rejected the worldly riches and abandoned the reigns of power when...   Religion/History/Biographies Pages 170

The Complete Works of Guy de Maupassant by *Guy de Maupassant*   ISBN: *1-59462-157-8* **$16.95**
"For days and days, nights and nights, I had dreamed of that first kiss which was to consecrate our engagement, and I knew not on what spot I should put my lips..."   Fiction/Classics Pages 240

The Art of Cross-Examination by *Francis L. Wellman*   ISBN: *1-59462-309-0* **$26.95**
Written by a renowned trial lawyer, Wellman imparts his experience and uses case studies to explain how to use psychology to extract desired information through questioning.   How-to/Science/Reference Pages 408

Answered or Unanswered? by *Louisa Vaughan*   ISBN: *1-59462-248-5* **$10.95**
Miracles of Faith in China   Religion Pages 112

The Edinburgh Lectures on Mental Science (1909) by *Thomas*   ISBN: *1-59462-008-3* **$11.95**
This book contains the substance of a course of lectures recently given by the writer in the Queen Street Hail, Edinburgh. Its purpose is to indicate the Natural Principles governing the relation between Mental Action and Material Conditions...   New Age/Psychology Pages 148

Ayesha by *H. Rider Haggard*   ISBN: *1-59462-301-5* **$24.95**
Verily and indeed it is the unexpected that happens! Probably if there was one person upon the earth from whom the Editor of this, and of a certain previous history, did not expect to hear again...   Classics Pages 380

Ayala's Angel by *Anthony Trollope*   ISBN: *1-59462-352-X* **$29.95**
The two girls were both pretty, but Lucy who was twenty-one who supposed to be simple and comparatively unattractive, whereas Ayala was credited, as her Bombwhat romantic name might show, with poetic charm and a taste for romance. Ayala when her father died was nineteen...   Fiction Pages 484

The American Commonwealth by *James Bryce*   ISBN: *1-59462-286-8* **$34.45**
An interpretation of American democratic political theory. It examines political mechanics and society from the perspective of Scotsman James Bryce   Politics Pages 572

Stories of the Pilgrims by *Margaret P. Pumphrey*   ISBN: *1-59462-116-0* **$17.95**
This book explores pilgrims religious oppression in England as well as their escape to Holland and eventual crossing to America on the Mayflower, and their early days in New England...   History Pages 268

www.bookjungle.com *email: sales@bookjungle.com fax: 630-214-0564 mail: Book Jungle PO Box 2226 Champaign, IL 61825*

QTY

The Fasting Cure *by Sinclair Upton* ISBN: *1-59462-222-1* **$13.95** ☐
In the Cosmopolitan Magazine for May, 1910, and in the Contemporary Review (London) for April, 1910, I published an article dealing with my experiences in fasting. I have written a great many magazine articles, but never one which attracted so much attention... New Age/Self Help/Health Pages 164

Hebrew Astrology *by Sepharial* ISBN: *1-59462-308-2* **$13.45** ☐
In these days of advanced thinking it is a matter of common observation that we have left many of the old landmarks behind and that we are now pressing forward to greater heights and to a wider horizon than that which represented the mind-content of our progenitors... Astrology Pages 144

Thought Vibration or The Law of Attraction in the Thought World ISBN: *1-59462-127-6* **$12.95** ☐
by William Walker Atkinson Psychology/Religion Pages 144

Optimism *by Helen Keller* ISBN: *1-59462-108-X* **$15.95** ☐
Helen Keller was blind, deaf, and mute since 19 months old, yet famously learned how to overcome these handicaps, communicate with the world, and spread her lectures promoting optimism. An inspiring read for everyone... Biographies/Inspirational Pages 84

Sara Crewe *by Frances Burnett* ISBN: *1-59462-360-0* **$9.45** ☐
In the first place, Miss Minchin lived in London. Her home was a large, dull, tall one, in a large, dull square, where all the houses were alike, and all the sparrows were alike, and where all the door-knockers made the same heavy sound... Childrens/Classic Pages 88

The Autobiography of Benjamin Franklin *by Benjamin Franklin* ISBN: *1-59462-135-7* **$24.95** ☐
The Autobiography of Benjamin Franklin has probably been more extensively read than any other American historical work, and no other book of its kind has had such ups and downs of fortune. Franklin lived for many years in England, where he was agent... Biographies/History Pages 332

Name	
Email	
Telephone	
Address	
City, State ZIP	

☐ **Credit Card**   ☐ **Check / Money Order**

Credit Card Number	
Expiration Date	
Signature	

Please Mail to: Book Jungle
PO Box 2226
Champaign, IL 61825
or Fax to: 630-214-0564

ORDERING INFORMATION

web: *www.bookjungle.com*
email: *sales@bookjungle.com*
fax: *630-214-0564*
mail: *Book Jungle PO Box 2226 Champaign, IL 61825*
or PayPal *to sales@bookjungle.com*

Please contact us for bulk discounts

DIRECT-ORDER TERMS

**20% Discount if You Order
Two or More Books**
Free Domestic Shipping!
Accepted: Master Card, Visa,
Discover, American Express

www.ingramcontent.com/pod-product-compliance
Lightning Source LLC
Chambersburg PA
CBHW081229090426
42738CB00016B/3240